England Scotland Republic of Ireland Northern Ireland Wales Brazil Germany Italy France Turkey Liverpool Arsenal Chelsea Everton Manchester United Middlesbrough Blackburn Rovers Tottenham Hotspur Newcastle United Leeds United Southampton Manchester City Fulham Aston Villa Birmingham City Sunderland Charlton Athletic West Ham United West Bromwich Albion Bolton Wanderers Portsmouth Leicester City Norwich City Watford Nottingham Forest Reading Sheffield United Coventry City Rotherham United Wolverhampton Wanderers Burnley Crystal Palace Derby County Gillingham Wimbledon Millwall Preston North End Walsall Bradford City Ipswich Town Grimsby Town Stoke City Sheffield Wednesday Brighton & Hove Albion Wigan Athletic Oldham Athletic Cardiff City Bristol City Crewe Alexandra Queens Park Rangers Brentford Blackpool Chesterfield Luton Town Tranmere Rovers Wycombe Wanderers Port Vale Northampton Town Stockport County Plymouth Argyle Barnsley Swindon Town Notts County Huddersfield Town Colchester United Peterborough United Cheltenham Town Mansfield Town Hartlepool United Rushden & Diamonds Bournemouth Torquay United Wrexham Kidderminster Harriers Cambridge United Scunthorpe United Lincoln City Bury Oxford United York City Southend United Hull City Shrewsbury Town Rochdale Macclesfield Town Leyton Orient Darlington Carlisle United Bristol Rovers Exeter City Boston United Swansea City Chester City Hereford United Workington Gretna Aylesbury United Bedlington Terriers Berkhamsted Town Taunton Town Barry Town Bangor City Coniston Ambleside United Ullswater United Barrow Rangers Celtic Hearts Dunfermline Athletic Hibernian Dundee Aberdeen Kilmarnock Livingston Partick Thistle Dundee United Motherwell Falkirk Inverness Caledonian Thistle St Johnstone Clyde Queen of South Ayr United Ross County St Mirren Arbroath Alloa Athletic Raith Rovers Stranraer Berwick Rangers Brechin City Forfar Athletic Dumbarton Cowdenbeath Airdrie United Hamilton Academicals Stenhousemuir East Fife Peterhead Albion Rovers Greenock Morton Stirling Albion Gretna Elgin City Montrose Queen's Park East Stirling Forres Mechanics Huntly Abbey Stadium Adams Road Aggborough Stadium Alderstone Road Anfield Ashton Gate Avenue Stadium Ayresome Park Baseball Ground Bay View Belle Vue Bescot Stadium Bloomfield Road Blundell Park Boghead Bootham Crescent Boothferry Park Borough Park Boundary Park Bower Fold Bramall Lane Brisbane Road Britannia Stadium Broadwater Brockville Brunton Park Buckingham Road Burnden Park Burslem Cappielow Carrow Road Celtic Park Christie Park City Ground Cliftonhill County Ground Craven Cottage Dean Court Deepdale Dell Den Dens Park Deva Stadium Douglas Park Dronfield East End Park Easter Road Eastville Edgar Street Edgeley Park Elland Road Elm Park Ewood Park Feethams Fellows Park Filbert Street Field Mill Firhill Fir Park Fratton Park Gay Meadow Gayfield Park Giant Axe Gigg Lane Glandford Park Goldstone Ground Goodison Park Gresty Road Griffin Park Haig Avenue Hampden Park Hawthorns High Park High Street Highbury Highfield Road Hillsborough Holker Street Home Park Huish Park Ibrox Stadium Irongate Ground JJB Stadium Kenilworth Road Kilbowie Park Kingsfield Road Layer Road Leeds Road Links Park Loftus Road London Road Love Street McAlpine Stadium McDiarmid Park Madejski Stadium Maine Road Manor Ground Meadow Lane Millennium Stadium Millmoor Molineux Moss Rose Nene Park Ninian Park Oak Tree Road Oakwell Old Trafford Ora Stadium Palmerston Park Head Parkside Road Pittodrie Plainmoor Plough Lane Portman Road Prenton Park Pride Park Priestfield Stadium Racecourse Ground Raydale Park Recreation Ground Reebok Stadium Riverside Rockingham Road Roker Park Roots Hall Rugby Park St Andrews St George's Lane St James' Park St Mary's Saltergate Sandy Lane Sealand Road Selhurst Park Shay Shepherdsbridge Sincil Bank Sixfields Spotland Springfield Park Stadium of Light Stamford Bridge Tannadice The Dell The Den The Hawthorns The Shay The Stadium The Valley Turf Moor Twerton Park Tynecastle Underhill University of Bath Upton Park Vale Park Valley Valley Parade Vetch Field Vicarage Road Victoria Ground Victoria Park Villa Park Walkers Stadium Watling Street Welfare Ground Wembley Whaddon Road White Hart Lane Windsor Park Going to the match Standing Seating Coach travel Sponsors Hoardings Turnstiles Corner-flags Disabled Stretchers Floodlights Mascots Shirts Boots Dugouts The Bench Tea-Rooms Burger Vendors Changing-Rooms Football Inflatables Tannoys Tunnels Exits Players Stewards First-Aid Commentators John Motson Referees Linesmen Managers Coaches Substitues Police Police Horses Police Dogs TV Coverage Radio Commentary BBC ITV Sport Radio Five Live Sky Sports Irish Football Scottish Football Welsh Football Women's Football Junior Football Playing-fields Icons Zidane Beckham Shearer McCoist Andy Cole Cantona Gascoigne Ronaldo Del Piero Vialli Keegan Bryan Robson Lineker Platt Waddle Graham Taylor Souness Martin O'Neill Dalglish George Graham Howard Wilkinson Joe Royle Jim Smith Alex Ferguson Sven-Goran Erickson Success Winning Losing Winners Losers Crying Laughing Singing Westmorland League Football League Nationwide Conference Nationwide League Premier League World Cup FA Cup Champions League

SPONSORED BY

IN ASSOCIATION WITH

football in our time

IN REPLICA KIT
SUNDERLAND 1999 (*cat. no. 4392*)

football in our time

A Photographic Record of Our National Game

stuart clarke

MAINSTREAM
PUBLISHING

EDINBURGH AND LONDON

First published in Great Britain in 2003 by
MAINSTREAM PUBLISHING COMPANY (EDINBURGH) LTD
7 Albany Street
Edinburgh EH1 3UG

ISBN 1 84018 736 0

Reprinted 2004

Typeset in Garamond and Stone

Scanning by Colour Connection, Glasgow

Printed in Great Britain by Butler & Tanner Ltd, Frome and London

Front Cover: SUNSET OVER SPRINGFIELD PARK
WIGAN ATHLETIC 1990 (*cat. no. 0201*)
The greatest spectacle of any? A game that will always be with us . . .

Back Cover: HIGH-KICKING CANTONA
MANCHESTER UNITED V. MANCHESTER CITY (*cat. no. 2213*)
United are storming all barricades . . . pushing City downwards.

Front Endpaper: THE TIME IS NIGH
READING 2003 (*cat. no. 6722*)
Reading have spent several seasons at their fantastic Madejski Stadium
just off the M4, but now could just be the time to step up to the Premier League for the very first time.

Back Endpaper: CARRY ON UP THE ACADEMY
WEST HAM UNITED V. MANCHESTER CITY 2002 (*cat. no. 6315*)

Page 1: LEANING FORWARD
LIVERPOOL 2002 (*cat. no. 6555*)

Contents

Introducing the Work of Stuart Clarke 8
The Sponsors 10

1. Camaraderie, Fraternity . . . and the Full Moon 11
2. We, the Fans 33
3. Never Let You Down 57
4. Sacred Ground 77
5. Made in England, Mostly 119
6. World Cup Tsunami 139
7. Back Home 179
8. Final Matches at Favourite Old Grounds 197

Me in My Time 233
The Great and the Good 235
Acknowledgements 240

HELD UP HIGH
EVERTON V. LIVERPOOL 2003 *(cat. no. 6651)*

HIGH NOON IN NORTH LONDON
ARSENAL V. LIVERPOOL 1990 (*cat. no. 0245*)
Liverpool are found wanting come the Christmas showdown in the battle for the Championship 'between north and south'. Football's powerbase is surely shifting to London for the new decade.

Introducing the Work of Stuart Clarke

FOURTEEN YEARS OF FOOTBALL HISTORY HAVE PASSED SINCE I STOOD WITH CAMERA IN HAND SOMEWHERE, probably on a street of old cobbles, perhaps 'up north', believing I and only I had been given a peculiar and privileged path to take.

This is the result of that path. A book of the best of my work in this field, a book of dreams.

I begin with photographs that expose the camaraderie and fraternity which makes man so special, something that, since David Attenborough is not so big on football, I've taken on. We are like 'Meerkats United' supporting our team. There is also something primal about us, hence my adding ' . . . and the Full Moon' to the title of the first chapter.

The second selection of pictures looks at 'the fan' slightly closer up, perhaps taken away from the madding crowd and looked at in isolation. Some crowds are surely made up of loads of one-offs who really prefer their own company, their thoughts, statistics and dreams.

There follows a section where I show how crowds of supporters and the lone fan can expect to be disappointed, whether by the failings of the team on the field or by problems off it. In the most tragic case, we get a Hillsborough scenario. Thank goodness for the Football Trust and now the Foundation, and indeed the clubs themselves, for making the grounds better and more safe.

Which brings us to the fourth chapter, entitled 'Sacred Ground' because for all the safety, there is still criticism directed at the so-called 'improvements' made to football grounds in the modern era. Have clubs gone too far, at the expense of the fan and his or her sense of tradition? No, they have not. We have to move on to bring on new fans and protect tradition.

The game that was born within these shores and exported well over a century ago has now changed, receiving fans and players who have come, in the opposite direction, in numbers. At any major match each week there will be hordes of Scandinavians and Danes, and possibly some French and Italians, in the crowd. They are joined now by Japanese, who have added Beckingham Palace to Wordsworth, Beatrix Potter and The Beatles as English things to absorb into their culture. The copycats! The game is rich with foreign players doing all the things our boys can do, with a bit of added verve, or at a cheaper price, which occasionally makes you wonder if there is anything in a name any more and whether supporting the team of your town is still an obvious/natural thing to do. Yes, it is – we all of us love where we came from, but surely we are allowed a second team as well?

Should you have an identity crisis, it is surely resolved every four years at the World Cup – *the* most-watched event on the planet. Just think of that. And just think of the deal that could be struck on the inter-planetary TV rights! In 2002 the football World Cup went to the other side of the Earth, to Asia, for the first time. In Japan, where England were based, a simple tournament became an unforgettable and unique one as the will of a relatively small nation took on the world. The Japanese are a lovely people and they consumed any would-be warring tribes with their friendliness, honesty and good humour. They reminded us what it is like to feel an absolute sense of belonging.

'Back Home' is the next section. This book is, above all, about the British game and after the holidays and the sun we have to remember that *this* is where it all began and *right here* is where it all began for most of us reading this book. Let's still be a bit precious about 'our' football, at least for a few more years.

'Final Matches at Favourite Old Grounds' is the last chapter. I am well aware that not all grounds were, or are, loved and that tomorrow's state-of-the-art ground will one day be history, built over with shops or a car park.

I can only apologise to anyone whose team has been left out of this selection – it's nothing personal.

The bit about me at the end gives you an insight into my psyche and background. I could have been tempted to rattle off technical stuff about what cameras I used but really the greater thing to think of is the heart of the work and the way we look at things. Which is why I have encouraged the great and the good to say a few lines about why they like certain pictures in the book and the collection.

Should you find that the book has whet your appetite for more, go and see one of my touring exhibitions or the permanent place open every day in the Lake District, where you can get the scale of some of the pictures. The nice thing about a book, however, is it's yours for keeps and you can open it up when you like. I'm a big fan of my own work and this book contains the best of it.

If I've left any out, it opens the door for a sequel. Thanks are given at the end.

Stuart Clarke, Ambleside
31 May 2003

GOOD OLD EAST END MANNERS
West Ham United 1990 (*cat. no. 0012*)

Sponsors

PETER GANDOLFI, HEAD OF SPORTS MARKETING, NATIONWIDE BUILDING SOCIETY

Nationwide is the world's largest building society and sponsors football at every level across England, Scotland, Wales and Northern Ireland. Stuart Clarke's pluralistic approach, with attention to quality and good nature, really captures the passion people feel about football in the UK. We really think this is a collection of pictures the nation can be proud of.

PETER LEE, CHIEF EXECUTIVE OF THE FOOTBALL FOUNDATION

The Football Trust and its successor body, The Football Stadia Improvement Fund, have helped to redevelop the country's football grounds. Every League club in the country has benefited from our grant aid. The Football Foundation's task now is to revitalise the grassroots of the game in our parks and schools. Stuart Clarke's pictures capture in splendid fashion the period of transformation of our League grounds.

GORDON TAYLOR, CHIEF EXECUTIVE OF THE PROFESSIONAL FOOTBALLERS ASSOCIATION

The PFA supports footballers past and present and well beyond their involvement in the game, helping them to retrain after what is a short career. The PFA also supports the wider community in which they are 'players'. Most footballers were once fans, growing up all over the UK and beyond, and in the pictures of Stuart Clarke we see many accents visually expressed that confirm the intimacy the game still enjoys with the people, whatever their background.

1. Camaraderie, Fraternity . . . and the Full Moon

WAITING ON THE MEN OF AYR
AYR UNITED 1997 (*cat. no. 2980*)
The men will be along soon.

Page 11: UNDER A SEPTEMBER SKY
WIGAN ATHLETIC 1990 (*cat. no. 0203*)

TRANMERE ROVERS ON THE MOVE
WEMBLEY 1991
(*cat. no. 0613*)
The weekend's trip to London for the play-off final has been successful.

ALMOST SETTLED ON THE KOP
LIVERPOOL 2002
(*cat. no. 6554*)
The match versus Manchester United unites the locals in a common cause.

NEON GIRLS
TRANMERE ROVERS 1992 (*cat. no. 0825*)
The queue to buy a burger and a cup of tea from the two sisters – a third is up the Cowsheds End
– offers a welcome break from the game, a dreary goalless affair versus Watford.

SHARING A SPORTING OCCASION
LIVERPOOL AT CARDIFF MILLENNIUM STADIUM V. ARSENAL 2002 (*cat. no. 5442*)
They are on the phone to someone.

ALLEGIANCE TO THE WALL
RANGERS AT HAMPDEN STADIUM V. CELTIC 1994 (*cat. no. 1410*)
Even though the national stadium has plush new toilets just yards away,
the brethren prefer to go the old way – it's in their genes.

THE H'AWAY THE LADS
NEWCASTLE UNITED AT IPSWICH TOWN 1990 (*cat. no. 0223*)
A rum bunch of Geordies, pregnant with the booze and the football,
descend on sleepy Suffolk on a mild September day.
The Toon are bottom of Division Two.

CUP OF CHEER IN THE RAIN

SUNDERLAND 1991 (*cat. no. 0549*)
It's April and the season is drawing to a close. The match versus Arsenal draws a big crowd – and the live-TV cameras. Sunderland are going down and Arsenal could be crowned Champions.

UNDER THE TOON MOON

NEWCASTLE UNITED 1993
(*cat. no. 1281*)
The elite are tucked up under the crinkly roof, protected from the moon.

GIRL FEELS A PART OF IT
SUNDERLAND 1991 *(cat. no. 0551)*

BOY FEELS A PART OF IT
SUNDERLAND 1991 *(cat. no. 0554)*

BOTTOMS UP
BARNSLEY 1997 (*cat. no. 3082*)
The impossible has become reality:
Barnsley have been promoted to the
Premier League. The town is on the
map for all the right reasons.

DRINKING RED CHAMPAGNE IN
T'TOWN SQUARE (UP THE REDS)
BARNSLEY 1997 (*cat. no. 3084*)
The drinking has begun and will
continue all through the summer
until the new season brings top-
flight football to . . . Barnsley.

FANZINE SELLER
ADJUSTS HER BUM-BAG
BARNSLEY 1997 (*cat. no. 3138*)
The crowd versus West Ham shall be a full house on this barmy, historic August day. For some time the loyal support has, self-mockingly, made out that watching Barnsley is on a par with watching Brazil . . . Today it seems ten times sexier.

FATHER & SON UP OAKWELL
BARNSLEY 1997 (*cat. no. 3139*)
It's the first day in the Premiership for Barnsley. No one in all of Barnsley history has seen this before. People have cancelled foreign holidays to be here. Some live a stone's throw away.

21

IN THE FORUM (FIGHTING RELEGATION)
NEWCASTLE UNITED AT IPSWICH TOWN 1990 (*cat. no. 0219*)
'*Hail Caesar*', '*Et tu, Brute?*' and all that.

ROMANCE OF EARLY SEASON
BURNLEY 1991 (*cat. no. 0631*)
A Lancashire Cup fixture in July versus Wigan Athletic. There's plenty of room in the top corner of the Longside beside the tea-hut.

BOWLER-HAT BRIGADE
NEWCASTLE UNITED AT SUNDERLAND 1991
(*cat. no. 0726*)
Sartorial elegance for the
Roker joker away day romp.

GOT THEM THIS FAR
BEDLINGTON TERRIERS 2001
(*cat. no. 5252*)
Up in Northumberland, the Terriers have had it all their own way for several seasons now, their superior spirit conquering all opposition. Today they face an unknown quantity in the shape of some 'soft' southerners from a club called Berkhamsted Town. They are one step away from the FA Trophy final (at Villa Park).

BOY ON HIS ROKER SWING
SUNDERLAND 1991 (*cat. no. 0545*)
A leg up at Roker Park.

BAIRDS OF BOGHEAD
DUMBARTON 1995 (*cat. no. 1907*)
The crowd have not asked for it . . . but they are in any case having their portrait made. Boghead will not always be here and nor will they – in whatever order.

NATION IN LOVE WITH BURNLEY
BURNLEY 2000
(*cat. no. 5045*)
On the way to the match
versus Portsmouth, via
the pub on the corner.

THROUGH THICK AND THIN
SWANSEA CITY 1994 (*cat. no. 1429*)
Opponents Fulham are already relegated to the bottom division and City are left to chase mid-table respectability – a far cry from when they almost ruled the land and waved their flag in Europe.

GREAT SHOWS OF COLOUR . . . AND VERSE
CELTIC V. RANGERS 1997 (*cat. no. 2989*)
The battle off the pitch is well underway.

POWERS THAT BE
WORKINGTON 2001 (*cat. no. 5330*)
The president is here, and seated.

MEN WITH ENERGY AND LOVE BITES
WORKINGTON 2001 (*cat. no. 5336*)
In one of only a few places in the UK, this ancient game is played out. The 'Uppies' have to get the ball in the castle grounds up the hill and the 'Downies' the ball in the harbour. The match takes as long as it takes (best of three). Anyone can play for either team. But don't let Grandad catch you on the wrong side.

FAMILY AND FAVOURS
YEOVIL TOWN V. RUSHDEN AND DIAMONDS 2001 (*cat. no. 5345*)
The season draws to a close and one of these two teams will be promoted to the Football League – in either case for the very first time. The TV cameras are here in Somerset.

VISITING FANS QUITE NAUGHTY
BURNLEY 1992 (*cat. no. 0943*)
Burnley are finally on their way to promotion, via a trip to Carlisle where they burst out of their pen and take over more than half the ground, dressed as elephants, beach bums . . . and St. Trinian's.

LIGHT SHINES ON A GENERATION
CELTIC 2000 (*cat. no. 5007*)
Nowhere in Britain is the camaraderie felt more deeply
and the idea of one big family more keenly rehearsed.

TENSION AMOUNTS ON THE KOP
BRADFORD CITY 2000 (*cat. no. 4794*)
The match versus Liverpool will decide the fate of both. For City it is
Premiership survival after their first season in it. And they are leading.

GOALKEEPERS' VIEW OF THE CROWD
MANCHESTER CITY AT BLACKBURN ROVERS 2000 (*cat. no. 4753*)
City have ridden their luck all the first half and suddenly there's a clutch of goals.
Indeed a fourth comes and promotion is theirs for the second season running.

HANDS HELD HIGH
CELTIC V. RANGERS 2000 (*cat. no. 5008*)
Needless to say which team has just scored another in the first derby of the season. It's a rout.

ON THE BUS WITH THE CUP
CELTIC V. RANGERS 1999 (*cat. no. 4438*)
On the way to the new Hampden, the green double-decker
crosses the path of a lowly blue car. The Hoops have already
laid claim to this Cup final (which Rangers will win).

BARMIEST FANS IN THE UK
(BASED ON MY EXPERIENCES AFTER
14 YEARS COMPILING *FOOTBALL IN OUR TIME*)

1. Glasgow Celtic
2. Portsmouth
3. Manchester City
4. Sunderland
5. Newcastle United
6. Stoke City
7. Wolverhampton Wanderers
8. Cardiff City
9. Norwich City
10.= Barnsley
10.= Birmingham City
10.= Bristol Rovers
10.= Chelsea
10.= Leeds United
10.= West Bromwich Albion

2. *We, the Fans*

**RED-STREAKED CHEEKS IN
THE WARM REFRESHMENT ROOM**
BEDLINGTON TERRIERS 2001 (*cat. no. 5249*)
Half-time and the match versus Berkhamsted is not going to script.
The warm spring sun holds some consolation.

GEORDIE CROWD OUTNUMBERS UNITED
NEWCASTLE UNITED V. MANCHESTER UNITED, WEMBLEY 1999 (*cat. no. 4427*)
They come in their hordes, the furthest distance of any, to Wembley, with the hope they
will do so much better than the previous year's final when they left with faces red.

MAN COME A LONG WAY
LIVERPOOL 1990 (*cat. no. 0047*)
Liverpool take on Chelsea at Anfield.
For some it's a pilgrimage.

PREPARING FOR A FEAST
SUNDERLAND 2002 (*cat. no. 5676*)
The disappointing season is coming
to an end, the worst behind them.
Liverpool are the opposition.
Sunderland will play well and it will
look like they have turned the corner.

TWO BY TWO
LEICESTER CITY 2001
(*cat. no. 5622*)
City, bottom of the table coming into spring, take on Sunderland, who aren't having a great season themselves.

EMBRACE
BARNSLEY 1997
(*cat. no. 3078*)
The first fan to greet promotion to the Premiership. Bullock shall give up more than his boots to memento-hunters by the time he has waltzed to the sanctity of the changing-room.

FEELING WELL AT HOME
ROTHERHAM UNITED 2002 (*cat. no. 6280*)
It's uncharted territory for United, riding high in the First Division. The picnic shall be at Millmoor.

TWO-WAY TICKET
CELTIC 1996 (*cat. no. 2167*)
Celtic have been second best (to Rangers) for nearly a decade. But try telling that to the new breed.

ON A DIFFERENT CORNER
ROTHERHAM UNITED 2002
(*cat. no. 6288*)
Who shall come to this sacred place on such a day?

DUMBARTON EARLY BIRDS
DUMBARTON 1995
(*cat. no. 2026*)
Not that the crowd (versus the Accies) shall be a big one, but it's good to claim one's spot on the corner.

MAINTAINING A SENSE OF HUMOUR (BELLYFUL OF BURSLEM)
PORT VALE 1991 (*cat. no. 0411*)
The match versus Watford has its moments – unintentional and otherwise. The men in grey and boiler suits are mostly friends and this is the thing they love most in life, despite their apparent indifference. The man with sunglasses left of centre will collapse and die the following week amidst the same bunch of friends, away at Rotherham, but his family are comforted that there is this reminder of him in his element.

IPSWICH GET THEIR END AWAY
PORTSMOUTH 1999 (*cat. no. 4508*)
The league leaders face a tricky visit to the south coast
early in a season that shall eventually, after much
emotion . . . result in promotion to the Premiership.

NOR-FOLK
NORWICH CITY AT WOLVERHAMPTON WANDERERS 2002 (*cat. no. 5735*)
Norwich have sneaked up on the rails and threaten to overhaul Wolves in the race to the Premiership, via the play-offs.

TYKE FASHION
BARNSLEY 1997
(*cat. no. 3070*)
South Yorkshire
could be added to
London, Milan and
Paris on the carrier-
bags.

LUCKY MAN
EVERTON 2001
(*cat. no. 5513*)
Surrounded by his
extended family in the
warm Goodison air.

SEVEN UP ST MARY'S
SOUTHAMPTON 2001 (*cat. no. 5523*)
A new stadium heralds a new era which heralds a new
audience. The Saints have made the break from the old
mercurial home at The Dell to the dock side –
the city's traditional font of power.

MARCHING IN THE ALTOGETHER
NORWICH CITY 2002 (*cat. no. 5758*)
Norwich make their first visit to a major final in more
than a generation.

REMEMBER
BIRMINGHAM
CITY V. NORWICH
CITY AT CARDIFF
2002
(*cat. no. 5766*)
It shall be like a
sparkler, a match to
thrill like no other in
this short life.

UPTON PARKERS
WEST HAM
UNITED 2002
(*cat. no. 6310*)
Old strips and new.
The results, however,
could be better.

HILLSBOROUGH MEMORIAL
LIVERPOOL 1990 (*cat. no. 0040*)
The morning after a memorial service in Liverpool's Stanley Park (the walk
between Anfield from Goodison), recalling those who died at a football match
some miles away in South Yorkshire the Easter before.

(Middle Picture)
REPORTING FROM THE GROUND
WYCOMBE WANDERERS 1990 (*cat. no. 0247*)
John Motson takes the mike live for a *Football Focus* bulletin at the
very moment snows sweep in across England, cancelling matches
everywhere. Including this one.

THE KOP
LIVERPOOL 1992 (*cat. no. 0791*)
Cheek, wit and wisdom on the nation's most legendary football terrace.

MOST SPORTING FANS IN THE UK
(BASED ON MY EXPERIENCES AFTER 14 YEARS
COMPILING *FOOTBALL IN OUR TIME*)

1. Liverpool
2. Sheffield Wednesday
3. Bradford City
4. Fulham
5. Preston North End
6. Arsenal
7. Queens Park Rangers
8. Blackburn Rovers
9. Stenhousemuir
10. Cardiff

PEEL BACK THE FLAG FOR FOUR O'CLOCK
SHEFFIELD WEDNESDAY V. MANCHESTER UNITED
1994 (*cat. no. 1693*)

Football has a new time – 4 p.m. on Sundays – to suit live-TV coverage (on Sky). Five years have passed since the away end (left) took the lives of mostly Liverpool fans. Sheffield Wednesday and Hillsborough have a chance to celebrate – they always combine to subdue the mighty Reds of Manchester.

PRE-MATCH, ANFIELD
LIVERPOOL 1996 (*cat. no. 2239*)

The fans have a regular routine in the build-up to the match, hob-knobbing with all and sundry, including the opposing fans, in various taverns around Anfield. Sometimes the opposing supporters agree to meet up and discuss their varying fortunes.

HOME-FIRES BURNING
READING 1990 (*cat. no. 0206*)
The end of Elm Park is drawing
near. A plan has been hatched
to move away.

EMERGING FROM THE DEEP
PRESTON NORTH END 2000
(*cat. no. 5128*)
After years in the scullery, friendly
proud PNE have a new
exuberance.

THE HORSE
BURNLEY V. BLACKBURN
ROVERS 2000 (*cat. no. 5155*)
Burnley's promotions and
Blackburn's relegation sets up the
first League derby between these
two in years. The streets are paved
with police and the away team's
name is not featured on the
hoardings, it just says
'Burnley v' . . .

COLE'S LOVE'S LABOUR'S LOST
MANCHESTER UNITED V. NEWCASTLE UNITED 2000 (*cat. no. 4988*)
The former hero on the Tyne grabs another and some of the crowd are turned against him.

COVERED IN COVENTRY GLORY
COVENTRY CITY 2000 (*cat. no. 4666*)
Keane is the new hero at Highfield Road.

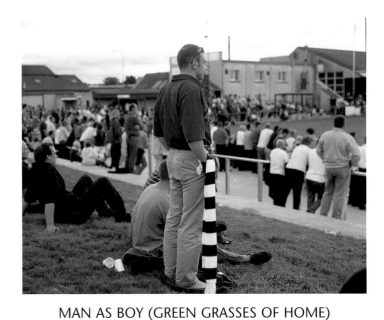

MAN AS BOY (GREEN GRASSES OF HOME)
ELGIN CITY 2000 (*cat. no. 4969*)
Elgin are the newest recruits to Division Three of the Scottish League. Now the giants of Highland football must mix it with the big boys from the south on a road that could lead anywhere.

JACK'S STATUTE
BLACKBURN ROVERS 2002 (*cat. no. 6230*)
A certain Walker will be remembered forever around Ewood for raising the stakes.

WHERE CROSS MEETS SCORER STREET
LINCOLN CITY 1999 (*cat. no. 4339*)
Approaching Sincil Bank, one is reminded of the most basic and effective of tactics. But do the Imps take heed?

WHY, WHY, WHY?
STOKE CITY 2000 (*cat. no. 4772*)
The song has been sung and the hail 'Delilah' conductor sinks back into the crowd . . . to watch
the match slip away in a fracas. 'Delilah', though not a 'football-song', goes some way to
explain the inexplicable passion aroused in fans by their football.

SIZE OF IT
ROCHDALE 2002 (*cat. no. 5661*)
Rochdale are unaccustomed to these big-
time occasions and tonight they have
Rushden to contend with for a trip to the
Third Division play-off final in Cardiff.

FANS GET ALL EXCITED (PART TWO)
BRADFORD CITY 2000 (*cat. no. 4799*)
Liverpool have been beaten and the season saved . . .
the grass is ever greener.

MAN WITH RADIO
ELGIN CITY V. HAMILTON ACADEMICALS 2000
(*cat. no. 4964*)
The man is experiencing at first hand the first
Marbles League fixture; albeit they are slipping
towards defeat. But still he wants to hear its every
nuance framed in the radio reporting of the day –
for this is history in the making.

THE WAITING (GAME)
ROTHERHAM UNITED
2002 (*cat. no. 6289*)

49

FRIENDS
BOLTON WANDERERS 1997 (*cat. no. 3133*)
Burnden Park is coming to an end with the match versus Charlton. So many memories, so many people who have known better and worse. Fathers, sisters, sons, grandads. All are here, today, stood at the same line in time. The end of an era and all that. Some will look at this photo in years to come, even today, and cry.

HOLKER GIRLS GET READY
BARROW 1998 (*cat. no. 3995*)
The coldest ground in the country greets a warm sea breeze.

CHELSEA STYLE SET
CHELSEA V. ARSENAL 2002 (*cat. no. 6270*)
Living up to the Kings Road legacy.

THE MENACE DISPERSED
DUNFERMLINE ATHLETIC AT DUNDEE UNITED 1996
(*cat. no. 2322*)
Escorted away from trouble by his wife, Dunfermline's
own Dennis the Menace is saved from the comic antics of
various Desparate Dans caked in Dundee disappointment.

51

52

Left: GASCOIGNE SEES A TRICK
TOTTENHAM HOTSPUR V. WIMBLEDON 1990
(*cat. no. 0233*)
Christmas approacheth and Gazza is in a playful
poise against Vinnie's Wimbledon outfit. The referee
plays his part.

CHRISTMAS CELEBRATIONS PREMATURE
MIDDLESBROUGH 1998 (*cat. no. 4188*)
The match versus Newcastle is interrupted by two half-naked Geordie Santas
heading for Gazza (now in Middlesbrough's colours).

FRATTON END LOOKS ON (PART ONE)
PORTSMOUTH 1999 (*cat. no. 4506*)
For now its just shouting and heckling and still within their armoury:
the biggest repertoire of songs of any set of fans. Why Portsmouth?
Who knows . . .

GISSA SNOG
EVERTON 2001 (*cat. no. 5514*)
The couple must enter via different gates,
but they will be reunited once inside at the tea-bar.

SECURE CAR PARKING

PORTSMOUTH 2001 (*cat. no. 5630*)
They shall be called stupid soft southerners
and they shall in turn – across a car park, road
or the length of a terrace – call visiting
Manchester City fans stupid thick
northerners. Fanatics all.

CRESTFALLEN

MANCHESTER UNITED AT
MANCHESTER CITY 2002
(*cat. no. 6468*)
Of all the games to go pale on. For red
shirts to pale to pink and for sky blue to
become onerous.

3. Never Let You Down

CITY OF FORTUNES
LIVERPOOL 1990 (*cat. no. 0160*)
What *is* 'winning' anyway?

COMMITTED TO THE LION'S DEN
MILLWALL 1990 (*cat. no. 0028*)
Millwall are already relegated by Easter, come the visit of goodie-two-shoes Lineker and his sidekick Gazza.

NEW HEADLINES TO BE MAKING
PORTSMOUTH 1992 (*cat. no. 0938*)

There is a tradition in Portsmouth, possibly since the War (when they remained Champions for all the time the League was suspended), to only take down the city's Christmas decorations once Pompey are out of the Cup. Which could be as late as April (or never) if they are to win it. Having lost at semi-final stage they receive the welcome of returning heroes, replete with those Xmas decorations tossed into the air as ticker-tape. A holy grail of sorts . . . to be continued.

WHAT IT TAKES TO PUT ON A MATCH
CARLISLE UNITED 1994 (*cat. no. 1700*)

CARLISLE BREAK A LEG
CARLISLE UNITED 1997
(*cat. no. 2945*)
United.

Opposite Page:

Top: **FANS STORM THEIR HEAVEN**
CARLISLE UNITED 1995 (*cat. no. 1786*)
Despite a mauling on the last day of the
season, United have provided one of the
best squads of Third Division Champions
in recent memory. A fact not lost on the
city.

Bottom: **TOAST OF THE TOWN**
CARLISLE UNITED 1995 (*cat. no. 1789*)
The tour through the streets on the open-
topped bus parading the Cup (and having
come close to the double at Wembley) is
much to be proud of for the chairman
Michael Knighton, who almost got hold of
Manchester United just seven seasons
before. Here in Carlisle he is a massive fish
in a smaller pond. 'The best day of my life,'
he declares.

SUPPORTER LOST AT SEA
CHESTER CITY 2000 (*cat. no. 4874*)
After minutes of not knowing, as so often happens on the last day of the season when it goes down to the wire, the truth is hollow. The Sealand Roaders are out of the League and the Great Escape (which looked on) is over.

ONE TREE ALBION
ALBION ROVERS 1992 (*cat. no. 0982*)
No one much ever comes to Cliftonhill.

FACING UP TO BANISHMENT
BRIGHTON AND HOVE ALBION AT HEREFORD UNITED
1997 (*cat. no. 3089*)
Of all the possibilities, how could it be that the two teams at the bottom of the entire League should find themselves drawn against each other on the final Saturday of the season? The defeated will lose their League status. No pressure!

HOPS AND CIDER REVIVER
HEREFORD UNITED V. BRIGHTON AND HOVE ALBION 1997
(*cat. no. 3086*)
The tradition of parading the bull ('with the big ones') around the pitch is continued even for this momentous game.

CHAIRMAN'S DREAM OF TOO MUCH ON HIS PLATE
CARLISLE UNITED 1993 (*cat. no. 1306*)

WAIT OF THE LEAGUE ON ONE'S SHOULDERS
BRIGHTON AND HOVE ALBION AT HEREFORD UNITED 1997
(*cat. no. 3092*)
The match played on the hangman's scaffold grows in intensity.

COMMANDING FIGURE CAPTURED ON FILM
BLACKBURN ROVERS V. NEWCASTLE UNITED 1993
(*cat. no. 1109*)
Kenny Dalglish is as easily understood from behind as from the Barry Davies position. But the laconic manager is in the process of bringing the Championship to unfashionable Blackburn the season after next.

HOPES RISE OVER CARLISLE
CARLISLE UNITED 2002 (*cat. no. 6208*)
The first day of the season and, after an Olympic interval of asking and trying, the city and the club are finally rid of their ogre and the sacked manager reinstated along with 10,000 fans (a crowd of 13,000 probably sets some sort of record). Carlisle will, however, again spend most of the season at the bottom.

ARRESTED BUT STAYING UP
BRIGHTON AND HOVE ALBION AT HEREFORD UNITED 1997
(*cat. no. 3099*)
The match of the decade goes to Brighton.
Hereford are out of the League.

CLINT'S CHANCE TO PUT BARNSLEY IN THE PREMIER
BARNSLEY V. BRADFORD CITY 1997 (*cat. no. 3075*)
Bradford need to win to ensure they stay up and Barnsley to
enter into a new stratosphere. A diminutive man from across the
Atlantic seals promotion. But within five years both clubs will be
in administration.

NAMES TO LOOK BACK ON
MIDDLESBROUGH 1991 (*cat. no. 0538*)
How could it have come to it that the once great club nearly
closed its doors just a few seasons before?
Now the glamour is surely returning.

UNCLE JOE ON THE WAY TO THE GROUND
WIGAN ATHLETIC 1997 (*cat. no. 2958*)
On the way to the ground, a reminder of one's lost youth.

TOMMY COOPER ROUTINE
OLDHAM ATHLETIC 1993 (*cat. no. 1134*)
Joe Royle takes a cushion out of the directors' box to protect his
shoes from the muddied pitch.

BORN OF SPRINGFIELD PARK
WIGAN ATHLETIC 1999 (*cat. no. 4413*)
The move to the JJB Stadium is weeks away.

FAT MAN TUCKS IT IN
NEWCASTLE UNITED AT IPSWICH TOWN 1990 (*cat. no. 0224*)
The mighty Quinn scoring freely for the struggling outfit, who
are bottom of Division Two.

NEVER GOING BACK
IPSWICH TOWN AT WEMBLEY 2000 (*cat. no. 4912*)
The match versus Barnsley will likely put Ipswich Town back in
the top flight, where they now believe they belong (though
until 1938 they weren't even in the League).

HEARTS IN THEIR MOUTHS
GREENOCK MORTON 1996 (*cat. no. 2369*)
The play-off versus Dundee United could put the Ton in the Premiership.

MET THEIR MATCH ON LOVE STREET
ST MIRREN 1995 (*cat. no. 1862*)

Out on the street, the local lads dressed in Rangers strips find other pursuits. This is the very town where Alex Ferguson as manager, armed with megaphone, drove around the shopping area on the back of a lorry shouting at the locals to support their St Mirren Football Club. Eventually he was sacked.

Top: FANS TAKE OVER (PART ONE)
CHESTERFIELD 2001 (*cat. no. 5405*)
Crowned Champions (of the Third Division), the last game of the season is a celebration. And a show of defiance . . .

Inset: HARRY HARRIS STAND
CHESTERFIELD 2001 (*cat. no. 5407*)
The national newspaper reporter is hated locally for having rubbished the town by suggesting the local football club were something akin to the town church's famous bent spire.

Below: FANS TAKE OVER (PART TWO)
CHESTERFIELD 2001 (*cat. no. 5406*)
At the height of their modest success, Chesterfield find themselves totally without directorship and chair following resignations in the wake of the scandal. Facing bankruptcy, the club is forced to put the entire promotion-winning squad on the market. Those wearing blue rosettes saying 'I am a director' are self-appointed stewards, using their local business skills to steer the club to safety.

Top left: SPIDER-WEB SMILER
CHESTERFIELD 2001 (*cat. no. 5408*)
The fan looks on the barmy day with entangled emotions – the almost melancholy of one's whole townsfolk outstreched before one – knowing that it is too good to last.

Top right: BAGGING ALL MANNER OF MEMENTOS
CHESTERFIELD 2001 (*cat. no. 5411*)
The youngsters claim that the Championship-winning players are their property. For keeps. This in the light of all the players being offered for sale.

Right: BLUE STEPS FROM OUTSIDE
CHESTERFIELD 2001 (*cat. no. 5397*)
The FA and Football League shall conduct their enquiries on what went on here. Chesterfield's promotion, meanwhile, goes ahead.

SALTER-GATE
CHESTERFIELD 2001
(*cat. no. 1786*)
A scandal of national implication, although relegated by the newsworthiness of greater clubs, concerning irregular payments, affixes itself to the Third Division Champions and threatens to sour and even disqualify their promotion.

GOING DOWN AT ROKER
SUNDERLAND V. NEWCASTLE UNITED 1992 (*cat. no. 1039*)
We, an island race, obsessed with our football, huddling shoulder to shoulder in all weathers, including a fine autumn
day . . . and suddenly the ball is whipped in and no one is yet celebrating save for he who has kicked it and the man up
the floodlight pylon who has an even better view for as long as he hangs on.

UP OR DOWN (THE END OF THE AFFAIR)?
ALDERSHOT 1990 (*cat. no. 0121*)
First they were told they were bust and then they were not. Then they were again. And most of the country have no idea that they are about to lose Aldershot from the Fourth Division.

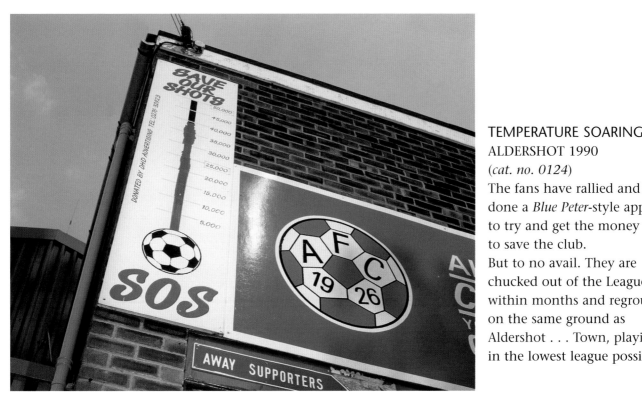

TEMPERATURE SOARING
ALDERSHOT 1990
(*cat. no. 0124*)
The fans have rallied and done a *Blue Peter*-style appeal to try and get the money in to save the club.
But to no avail. They are chucked out of the League within months and regroup on the same ground as Aldershot . . . Town, playing in the lowest league possible.

TIARA AND TUTU TIRADE
WOLVERHAMPTON WANDERERS 2002 (*cat. no. 5666*)
Having led the pack for the whole season – at one point being
way ahead and practically promoted – the Wolves have blown
it yet again. Now, through the play-offs, they have a chance
to turn it around. But they may have to wait one year for the
three goals.

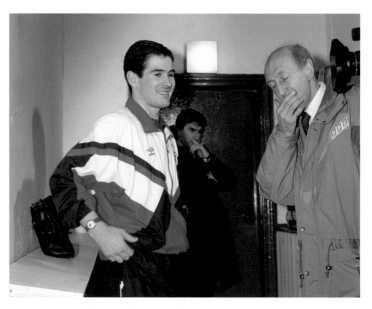

BARRY DAVIES CONSOLES YOUNG CLOUGH
NOTTINGHAM FOREST AT PORTSMOUTH 1992 (*cat. no. 0885*)
Forest have come to the South Coast and been dumped out of
the Cup. Father will not be pleased.

CLOSING THE CHINK
WOLVERHAMPTON WANDERERS 1993 (*cat. no. 1178*)
Four years on from almost biting the dust, Molineux is under
repair as a rich and famous person recalls he once lived
hereabouts.

CHANCE MEETING IN THE PARK
NOTTINGHAM FOREST 1991 (*cat. no. 0483*)
More eccentric by the minute, and particularly during that
pressured time waiting for kick-off, the great master manager
looks for someone on his level.

GENERAL GRANT SUMMONS HIS TROOPS
WOLVERHAMPTON WANDERERS 2002 (*cat. no. 5665*)
Wolves must win. They must get promoted.
Everybody knows that.

SPOT OF RESPECT AFTER THE GAME
STOKE CITY 1998 (*cat. no. 3381*)
Through the streets of Burslem run the City braves, proving
they are the men of the moment.

NEW MAN WITH THE BAG
SOUTHAMPTON 2001 (*cat. no. 5529*)
The Dell is gone and the fans are being asked to feel a part of
the new set up down at the old St Mary's.

WAITING FOR THE PLAYERS
BARNSLEY AT HUDDERSFIELD TOWN 2002 (*cat. no. 6297*)
One or even both of these Yorkshire clubs – giants just
yesterday – could slip to the bottom division at this rate,
unless someone pulls their finger out. Not that 'we' care
about Huddersfield.

GOD COMES DOWN
BURNLEY 2001 (cat. no. 5539)
Burnley boys struggle to come to terms with their status.

MOST LEGENDARY SLEEPING GIANTS IN THE UK
(BASED ON MY EXPERIENCES AFTER
14 YEARS COMPILING *FOOTBALL IN OUR TIME*)

1. Accrington (Stanley)
2. Wolverhampton Wanderers
3. Burnley
4. Hull City
5. Cardiff City
6. Bristol City
7. Plymouth Argyle
8. Milton Keynes (United)
9. Tottenham Hotspur
10. Carlisle United

LINE OF A SONG (TOILET HUMOUR)
CARLISLE UNITED 2002 (*cat. no. 5664*)
Having been unsaddled and put his son in charge, the man at the top has
become the man at the bottom – all respect lost. You try to do something
for the town and this is all the thanks you get! It will take a lord or higher
to broker a deal for the safe sell-on of the club!

MIDLAND'S SEMI-FINAL VENUE
ASTON VILLA 1990 (*cat. no. 0015*)
The greatest semi-final ever? I went outside to catch the mood, wondering
what the gods might be making of all this human chapter at the football ground.

4. Sacred Ground

EXIT FROM BLOCK A
NOTTS COUNTY 1990 (*cat. no. 0282*)
A huge funeral is taking place. Football is passing through.

FOG HAS LIFTED ON THE VALLEY
CHARLTON ATHLETIC 1990 (*cat. no. 0021*)
Abandoned beside the Thames and the new Thames flood barrier,
the mighty Valley doubts it shall ever be employed again.

FOG ON THE WEAR
SUNDERLAND 1991 (*cat. no. 0719*)
Man cometh across a landmark he knows well. He is bound for Roker Park, happed in mist.

LOYAL SUPPORT
NOTTS COUNTY 1990 (*cat. no. 0093*)
'Ome Bewer' it reads across the old stand. The oldest in the country.

SET IN STONE
OLDHAM ATHLETIC 1990 (*cat. no. 0179*)
Zoe makes sure she goes down in history . . . years before fans are invited to 'buy a name-brick' in the new stadia.

CORACLE TO FETCH THE BALL
SHREWSBURY TOWN 1991 (*cat. no. 0295*)
Should the ball be hoofed over the stand into the fast-flowing River Severn, the Coracle family will try and collect it.

WHAT OUR GRANDFATHERS SAW
BARNSLEY 1995 (*cat. no. 1842*)
The mainstand was well-crafted by Barnsley craftsmen back in the days when football was young. Even younger than today.

BAGGIES BAGGED TONIGHT
WEST BROMWICH ALBION V. SWANSEA CITY 1993 *(cat. no. 1165)*
A barmy night at The Hawthorns for the Second Division play-off with Swansea City.
The fans have taken over the scoreboard – but the result shall stand.

SUPER FREE-KICK IN STORE
BOLTON WANDERERS 1990 (*cat. no. 0048*)
On the very spot where tragedy once struck, Bolton have
allowed Normid to purchase a corner of the ground to build a
superstore, making for one of the most surreal sites in football.
All now a car park. The Wanderers having gone up the road to
the Reebok.

TEMPTATION OF THE TEA-GIRL
ST MIRREN 1995 (*cat. no. 1856*)
A seductive sun shines on a new season at St Mirren,
the Paisley club with the ground at Love Street.

MAXWELL HOUSE
OXFORD UNITED 1990 (*cat. no. 0030*)
The menu at the Maxwell family's football fortress, The
Manor, on the edge of Oxford.

WHERE PEOPLE MATTER
KILMARNOCK 1994 (*cat. no. 1326*)
They will soon all be made to sit down,
in a new shiny stand built by Barr.

ERSTWHILE CLUB SHOP
ALLOA ATHLETIC 1996 (*cat. no. 2278*)
Finally Alloa get to open a new, albeit similar-sized club shop,
freeing up the old one.

Most Memorable British Grounds No Longer Here
(BASED ON MY EXPERIENCES AFTER
14 YEARS COMPILING *FOOTBALL IN OUR TIME*)

1. Craven Cottage, Fulham
2. Ayresome Park, Middlesbrough
3. Baseball Ground, Derby County
4. Leeds Road, Huddersfield Town
5. Burnden Park, Bolton Wanderers (pre-Normid superstore)
6. Broomfield, Airdrieonians
7. Brockville, Falkirk
8. Roker Park, Sunderland
9. Boghead, Dumbarton
10.=Boothferry Park, Hull City
10.=The Dell, Southampton
10.=The Den, Millwall
10.=Wembley Stadium

SPION KOP SIGN
NOTTS COUNTY 1990 (*cat. no. 0094*)
The word 'Kop' apparently comes from South Africa where many
of Britain's first football supporters were engaged in the Boer War.
Enthusiastically they brought the name back to this other arena
where one man stands shoulder to shoulder with the next . . .
battalions of loyal supporters.

LAYER UPON LAYER OF SUPPORT
COLCHESTER UNITED 2002 (*cat. no. 6351*)
People's names all over the concourse. All the clubs are doing it,
but every brick is special to someone.

FRATTON I'LL RECALL
PORTSMOUTH 2000 (*cat. no. 4708*)
The historic station beside the historic ground.

GRAFFITI IN THE SHAGGING STAND
DALBEATTIE STAR 1996 (*cat. no. 2297*)
The ground sees some sort of action most nights of the week.

. . . ON LOVE STREET
ST MIRREN 1996 (*cat. no. 2913*)
In the glare of the headlamps.

V. DUNFERMLINE AT CAPPIELOW
GREENOCK MORTON 1995 (*cat. no. 1950*)
The Ton shall see off the League leaders on a memorable day with,
it must be said, few visiting supporters in attendance.

LIGHTS ON HIGH OVER ELLAND ROAD
LEEDS UNITED 1991 (*cat. no. 0737*)
Elland Road boasts the tallest floodlights in Europe. And diamond-shaped ones to boot.

BARROW V. CHESTER CITY IN THE FA CUP
BARROW 2001 (*cat. no. 5600*)
Dumped out of the League in the 1970s, Barrow have the chance of some FA Cup glory.

THE KOP THOUGHT QUIET
LIVERPOOL 1993 (*cat. no. 1195*)
The most famous Kop in all the world, falling silent.

GOODNIGHT GOODISON
EVERTON 1995 (*cat. no. 2049*)
A founder member of the Football League still at home in the heart of Goodison.
One day the club will surely relocate.

A TEST OF SPEED
SOUTHAMPTON 2001 (*cat. no. 5461*)
The Dell is a scuttling ground for many reputations. The Saints international all-stars take Man United
to task in the penultimate game ever at the awkward old homely ground.

Left: THE GATE IS SWUNG
BURNLEY 1990
(*cat. no. 0033*)
Burnley were there when the
Football League was born.

Right: PHYSIO GHOSTS
THROUGH THE
CORRIDORS
BURNLEY 1991
(*cat. no. 0427*)

SECRETS
LOCKED
AWAY
BURNLEY
1990
(*cat. no. 0181*)

TERRACING
ON TURF
MOOR
BURNLEY
1990
(*cat. no. 0050*)

Left: SPLATTERED CLARET
LEAVES THE TABLE
BURNLEY 1991
(*cat. no. 0438*)

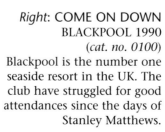

Right: COME ON DOWN
BLACKPOOL 1990
(*cat. no. 0100*)
Blackpool is the number one
seaside resort in the UK. The
club have struggled for good
attendances since the days of
Stanley Matthews.

Left: GLOW OF THE OLD BLACKBURN ROVERS 1992 (*cat. no. 0961*) Another of the founder members of the Football League.

Right: ARRIVAL OF JACK WALKER
BLACKBURN ROVERS
1992
(*cat. no. 0959*)
Having made his money in Blackburn, employing seemingly half the town, his money can now be put to further good use . . .

Left: AS SEEN THROUGH THE FLOODLIGHTS BLACKBURN ROVERS 1993 (*cat. no. 1313*) Ewood Park undergoes transformation with the millions invested by Jack Walker.

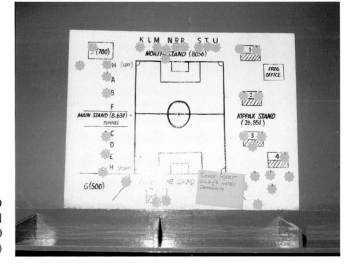

Right: OLD £5 GROUND PLAN
MANCHESTER CITY 1990
(*cat. no. 0194*)

Left: ANOTHER FEATURE OF THE MAINSTAND BURY 1990 (*cat. no. 0172*)

Right: WARM WELCOME
BLACKPOOL 1990
(*cat. no. 0104*)

IN PURSUIT OF THE TITLE AT SHEPHERDSBRIDGE
CONISTON V. STAVELEY 1999 (*cat. no. 4365*)

Once upon a time the mountain clattered with the sound of clogs (workmens' boots). On a Friday – particularly, being payday – the men were extra hurried in their escape from the mines all over the 'Old Man'. In the village hall, the clattering would continue. First to the sound of the men arriving – to see if they were in Saturday's team. And then to the sound of dancing, as those who weren't in the team expended their energies. The mountain is mostly quiet now. The clogs are put away. The dancing legacy lives on only at Shepherdsbridge Ground . . .

BEGINNINGS OF A FOREST
NOTTINGHAM FOREST 1993
(*cat. no. 1180*)
Close season and the lazy
suntanned grounds bask beneath
shady trees aside the beach.

LENGTHS AN ALBION FAN WILL GO TO
BRIGHTON AND HOVE ALBION AT MIDDLESBROUGH 1991
(*cat. no. 0542*)
They have travelled the lengths of the land. And now they have
burst through the perimeter fence to be with their Albion.

CLOUGH'S CHANGING-ROOM
NOTTINGHAM FOREST 1994 (*cat. no. 1366*)
The team is on the decline. Brian Clough's legacy is being wound
down. It shall be years before the club get over having had an
almost godlike figure tread their boards.

ALL SET FOR A NEW ERA
WEST BROMWICH ALBION 1992 (*cat. no. 0994*)
The Woodman Corner scoreboard-with-a-throstle-on-top survives a
safety inspection. Given some alterations. To have taken it down
entirely would have really annoyed the fans – as it is 'theirs'.

DOWNHILL FROM A CORNER
HEATHWAITE 1997 (*cat. no. 2969*)
The new team finds a green corner aside Lake Windermere
to start an ascent up the Westmorland League.

ENTRANCE-FEE REVIEW
ARBROATH 1996 (*cat. no. 2764*)
Sye Webster brought fame to the club when he ran on and kissed
the referee fully on the lips after a rousing Cup victory. With a
crowd of hundreds he didn't go unnoticed and was banished from
Gayfield Park. For 14 long months. During which time he
infamously got a sore bottom (piles) from sitting on the brick wall
with the vantage-point across from the ground. His legend lives on
in England at Ambleside Football Museum where there is a life-size
papier-mâché sculpture of Sye and his weeping wall.

HUGE ATTENDANCE SIDELINED
DALBEATTIE STAR 1996 (*cat. no. 2296*)

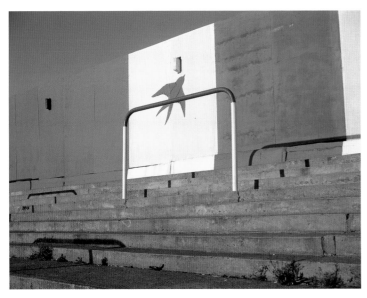

BLUEBIRD'S PLACE
BARROW 2001 (*cat. no. 5521*)
They put up a stand for improvement. Then it wasn't up to the safety standard. So they took it down. They were no good when they were in the League but now, when doing well outside the League, they want to be back in the League, where they will undoubtedly struggle again, if not be relegated. The flight back to where you think you want to be is full of obstacles.

ROUNDING THE CORNER
STOKE CITY 1991 (*cat. no. 0713*)
One of the original 12 League clubs – aptly playing at the Victoria Ground, the corner of which can be seen from the dual-carriageway. The plot to move to a 'Britannia Stadium' half a mile away, has not yet even been hatched.

SEAT FOR MR ALGAR
TORQUAY UNITED 1998 (*cat. no. 4070*)
Besides Algar, season ticket holders
include Mr Hair and Mr Lippie.

POLICE PATROL
WIGAN ATHLETIC 1990 (*cat. no. 0193*)

DANNY FACES THE PRESS
BARNSLEY 1998 (*cat. no. 3474*)
They came up the divisions and now they are at the summit
of their achievement – at the foot of the Premier League –
with only a few games to go of their first ever season
upstairs. A season that started out as fun, with 'nothing to
lose' (everybody said), threatens now to sink the club into
debt and rob the affable manager of his job (if only they
knew it).

CRIMSON TROPHY
BRISTOL CITY 1990 (*cat. no. 0211*)
In 1986, City of Ashton Gate won a minor major trophy for
the red half of the city. But for the rest of their history
someone has surely been asleep.

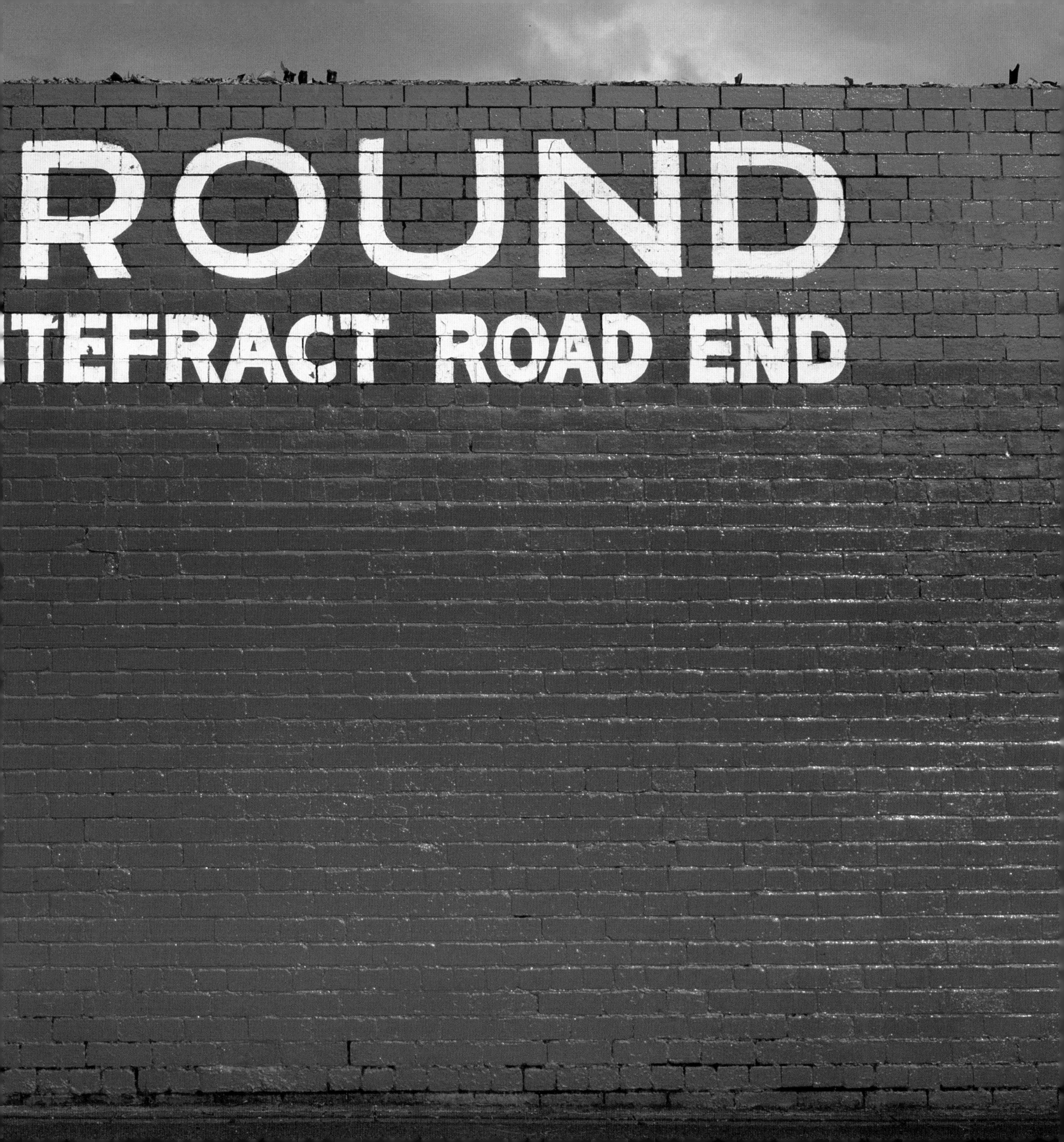
ROUND
TEFRACT ROAD END

FINDING A GAP
TOXTETH 2000 (*cat. no. 4974*)
Summer sees a series of tournaments for the boys on the estates.

CRACK AT BELLE VUE
DONCASTER ROVERS
1990 (*cat. no. 0218*)
A peak at the ground of
England's consistently
worst (Football League)
team. A sort of shock
value. A chamber of
football horrors. Years
later, after arson and
expulsions, including
their own from the
League, crowds gather
and performances pick
up. The Rovers are now
the Manchester United
of non-league.

HAPPINESS WAS BORN A TWIN
ROTHERHAM UNITED 2000 (*cat. no. 4642*)

THOSE HARD, COLD BENCH SEATS
CHELSEA 1996 (*cat. no. 2793*)
The recipe surely for rude bad health.

YELLOW BRICK ROAD
BRADFORD CITY 1992 (*cat. no. 1000*)
The golden yellow steps symbolise a path for football away from the bad old days. And here particularly – at Valley Parade – from the memory of a fire that killed unsuspecting fans one spring Saturday in 1985.

LET NO MAN MISTAKE HIS PLACE
ROTHERHAM UNITED 1998 (*cat. no. 4193*)
Millmoor competes for 'the grittiest in the land' label, where
men are men and excuses not harboured. Where a referee,
manager and all the players are made aware of their each and
every failing. At Rotherham, from the terrace perspective, they
will see it merely as 'banter', if not 'bonding'.

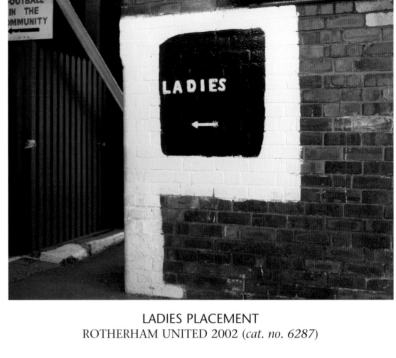

LADIES PLACEMENT
ROTHERHAM UNITED 2002 (*cat. no. 6287*)

COMPS COLLECTION WINDOW
HARTLEPOOL UNITED 1998 (*cat. no. 4117*)
Not too many takers at Victoria Park.

TO THE ROOM UPSTAIRS
COLCHESTER UNITED 2002 (*cat. no. 6347*)
The bouncer, black-eyed, bruised, economical with any
greeting, shows the VIPs to their safe-haven above Layer Road.

WHERE THE TEAM ARE BRIEFED
DONCASTER ROVERS 1991 (*cat. no. 0381*)

Just out of shot, legend Billy Bremner smokes another cigarette, feet up on his papers, letters, transfer requests, bills and phone-me-backs stick-it dockets, wondering just what it is he can do for the Rovers. He has played at the highest level, against world names, but his Doncaster outfit has Hartlepool, Colchester and Rochdale to contend with.

READY FOR TAKE OFF
MILTON KEYNES LADIES 1993 (*cat. no. 1266*)
The ladies have the changing-rooms for their FA Cup encounter.
Without a men's team of note in the city – the nearest League
team is some 20 miles away – a marketing man might get hold of
women's football here and make Milton Keynes a Manchester
United of women's football.

WALKING ALL OVER
BLACKPOOL 1990 (*cat. no. 0197*)
Back in the 1920s, women's football took off and attracted huge crowds.
Then the men that ran the game looked at each other and decided
against it.

DAWN FENCING
WIGAN ATHLETIC 1992 (*cat. no. 0947*)

PER-FIT PERFOMERS
ROCHDALE 2002 (*cat. no. 5660*)
The Rochdale versus Rushden play-off semi brings a touch of
unaccustomed glamour and media coverage to Spotland. And
between them, players all on the night, they milk the moment.

OLD CHANGING-ROOMS

CHESTER-LE-STREET 2003 (*cat. no. 6603*)

All over this part of the world footballers were born into less-than-ideal surroundings. Which were in turn the perfect settings for producing almost-perfect footballers. An inordinate number of players have emerged from this coal-seam.

PRIZED GROUND
AMBLESIDE UNITED 1998 (*cat. no. 4018*)
This heart of the Lake District is mostly in National Trust hands,
for the enjoyment of people everywhere. But this doesn't stop a
businessman from Blackpool buying up a piece of it and getting
into an unholy row with the neighbouring football club who have
to cross his land to get to where they have been for more than a
century.

GREEN AND PLEASANT
LANDING
AMBLESIDE UNITED 1997
(*cat. no. 3244*)
The Mountain Rescue
helicopter whirrs into
action just as the game
reaches a crescendo, in
this quiet, sacred corner.

IN DEFENCE OF THE REALM
KESWICK 1997 (*cat. no. 3267*)
Traffic is welcome. But restricted.

STROLLING TO THE OLD VILLA
ASTON VILLA 1992 (*cat. no. 1087*)
One of the original League clubs back in the 1880s. Time stands still here – no need to panic or even hurry. The Villa are going nowhere.

Opposite page: BURGER VENDOR
ARSENAL 1990 (*cat. no. 0246*)
Traditional fayre on the way home.

OLD MUSEUM PIECE
PRESTON NORTH END 1992 (*cat. no. 0895*)
Another one of the original League clubs. In years to come this same corner shall become the site for 'The National Football Museum', Preston proving their credentials ahead of Carlisle and any other runners and riders.

WRAP OF OLD HAMPDEN
SCOTLAND 1992 (*cat. no. 0981*)
This was an almighty ground, boasting the all-time highest UK attendance. And now it is in limbo, out of sorts with the move towards all-seater stadia. A relocation is out of the question and total refurbishment likely to break the Bank of Scotland. How *did* it turn out?

ON ICE
ENGLAND V. CAMEROON AT WEMBLEY 1991 (*cat. no. 0328*)
The coldest day this century awaits the first visit to London by an African national team.

VIEW FROM THE TERRACE
SUNDERLAND 1990 (*cat. no. 0108*)
In 1966 Roker Park staged World Cup games and people came from all over to walk these narrow streets and back-alleys. The stadium would not be considered again.

116

TERRACE AND STAND
CARDIFF CITY 1993 (*cat. no. 1197*)
Ninian Park once welcomed back their team as FA Cup holders. The only time
the Cup has left England – save perhaps for when it was stolen. As well as in
recent years when the finals have been staged at Cardiff's Millennium Stadium.

RED WELCOME ON THE WEST COAST
BERGEN 1997 (*cat. no. 2982*)
Liverpool arrive on the West Coast of Norway where they
(and Manchester United) are revered.

117

LEETLE BIT OF NAUGHTINESS (CANTONA STYLE)
MANCHESTER UNITED AT LEEDS UNITED 2001 (*cat. no. 5238*)

Barthez has clipped the back of an opponent, off camera. But the referee has indeed seen it, having eyes in the back of his head. The squeaky-clean Stam and Beckham come to the goalie's defence. Cantona would have loved the moment.

5. Made in England, Mostly

GET SADDAM CAFÉ
ARSENAL 1991 (*cat. no. 0310*)
The faces of Arsenal favourites are plastered all over the café wall, across from the ground. Other, newer players, some foreign, make the back pages now.

FOOTBALL LEAGUE CHAMPIONS
ARSENAL 1991
(*cat. no. 0578*)
George Graham has brought out the best of a middle-weight squad to take the title.

JOINING IN THE CELEBRATION
ARSENAL 2002 (*cat. no. 6399*)
Big-screen football comes to Highbury, reinforcing the sense of 'I was there to see it'. Highlights are played back at every opportunity.

HIGHBURY WAY
ARSENAL 2002 (*cat. no. 6397*)
Arsenal have suffered a rare setback. But it's still an incredibly sexy season around Highbury.

CANTONA'S CORRECTIVE PENALTY
MANCHESTER UNITED 1996 (*cat. no. 2212*)
A Frenchman called Eric, with his collar turned up in customary defiance, sends rivals City to the
foot of the table on their own patch. And tumbling towards relegation.

123

EBB & FLOW

GRIMSBY TOWN 1993 (*cat. no. 1238*)

An oil tanker rides the tide. And some of the crowd are happy watching this. Grimsby Town
meanwhile play Watford on the patch of green aside the Humber.

REBEL ROUSERS
MANCHESTER UNITED 2002 (*cat. no. 6511*)
The players are tied to one another with string, working for a common cause
and united under a humbling yet inspiring manager.

DUTCH WOMEN
HOLLAND AT ASTON VILLA, EURO '96 (*cat. no. 2453*)

MANAGER AND HIS CHARGES (STAGE LEFT)
CHELSEA AT SOUTHAMPTON 2001 (*cat. no. 5532*)
The calm Italian takes control of the inconsistent, globetrotting Chelsea
all-stars in an attempt to get them to knuckle-down and win the
Championship at the first or second or third or fourth attempt . . . it may
take him some seasons. Should Chairman Bates grant him that long?

LITTLE LIGHT RELIEF
SHEFFIELD UNITED 1997 (*cat. no. 3150*)

MEETING OF MINDS
ENGLAND AT BOLOGNA, ITALIA '90 (*cat. no. 0250*)
The English, and the Italians, have their work cut out
understanding one another. One thing is clear-cut: all are
here for the bother.

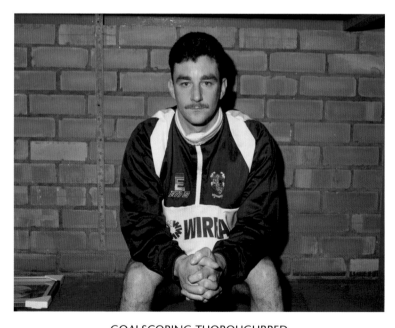

GOALSCORING THOROUGHBRED
TRANMERE ROVERS 1992 (*cat. no. 0827*)
The skinny-legged Aldridge has crossed the Mersey where he shall break
more scoring records and in so doing extend his playing career beyond the
mere 'few years at the top'.

SHEARER'S CHEEK
ENGLAND V. GERMANY AT CHARLEROI, EURO 2000
(*cat. no. 4901*)
The talismanic captain won't be shafted out of this match.
He's already scored one.

GAZZA COMES DOWN
TOTTENHAM HOTSPUR AT LEEDS 1990
(*cat. no. 0036*)
Gazza has endured the wrath of the home-team
support. Now he has to answer the press.

SHORT OFFENSIVE (IN THE CITY OF SAUCE)
ENGLAND V. BELGIUM AT BOLOGNA,
ITALIA '90 (*cat. no. 0251*)

JONES V. ARMFIELD AT OLD TRAFFORD
BBC RADIO, EURO '96 (*cat. no. 2556*)
The commentator and his summariser run the rule over
Europe's best.

DUTCH MAN
HOLLAND V. SCOTLAND AT ASTON VILLA,
EURO '96 (*cat. no. 2454*)
Possibly the tallest nation in the Western world.
With the elite of footballers.

BIG FASH AND SAM HAM DO THE WALK OF THE CAR PARK
WIMBLEDON 1990 (*cat. no. 0004*)
The Wimbledon phenomenon is in full swing,
masterminded by the chairman and his captain. In the
Plough Lane car park.

CLOSE EYE ON THE FINAL APPROACH
TOTTENHAM HOTSPUR V. COVENTRY CITY 1999 (*cat. no. 4525*)
Decisions and moves that shape a season are forged in seconds split.

FISTFUL OF DELILAH
STOKE CITY 2000 (*cat. no. 4764*)

WITH CANTONA IN MIND
MANCHESTER UNITED 2002 (*cat. no. 6510*)

IRON-MAN IRONY ALL-YORKSHIRE DERBY
SHEFFIELD UNITED V. LEEDS UNITED 1990 (*cat. no. 0166*)
The hard-man of football, ex-Wimbledon, having swapped clubs during
the summer, gets thumped by his own teammate. Years later he will make
his name in the movies behind a double-barrelled smoking shotgun.

CHELSEA IN BOLD
CHELSEA 2002 (*cat. no. 6272*)

GRASS-ROOTS GATHERING
FOOTBALL FOUNDATION AT THE COLLINS SPORTS CENTRE,
LIVERPOOL 2002 (*cat. no. 6235*)
Another generation of hopefuls from the streets of Merseyside. Granted, improved facilities. The search is on for home-grown talent to take on the world.

RULE BRITANNIA RISING
STOKE CITY V. CARDIFF CITY 2002 (*cat. no. 5721*)
Stoke's new stadium hosts old-style support – the most English of any in the whole of England? Cardiff have brought a fair few fans along to contest . . . everything.

SHIRTS ON THE LINE
READING 1990 (*cat. no. 0205*)
Elm Park hangs out its washing.

129

GUNNERS AGAINST RACISM
ARSENAL 2002 (*cat. no. 6395*)
English Football shows its true colours.

WINNING LEAGUE LINE-UP

LEEDS UNITED 1992 (*cat. no. 0952*)

In 1967, Glasgow Celtic won the European Cup with a team all born within 28 miles of Glasgow. Leeds have a couple of Yorkshiremen in their League-winning side of 1992, plus a Frenchman brought over by the manager.

ENGLAND AND GERMANY LINE-UP
WEMBLEY, EURO '96 (*cat. no. 2680*)
On the very same spot the World Cup winners stood 30 summers before.

GAZZA'S KILLER GOAL
WEMBLEY, EURO '96 (*cat. no. 2542*)
Seaman saves a Scottish penalty and within seconds Gazza is unleashed up the other end, to stunning effect.

ENGLAND EXPECTS . . . OPPOSITION
ENGLAND AT CHARLEROI, EURO 2000 (*cat. no. 4934*)
Many of the travelling support had taken in the battlefields of previous wars during their stay. With a win over the Germans in their boxer shorts, it is now party-time versus the humble Romanians.

Best International Support
(BASED ON MY EXPERIENCES AFTER
14 YEARS COMPILING *FOOTBALL IN OUR TIME*)

1. England
2. Holland
3. Mexico
4. South Korea
5. Argentina
6. Brazil
7. Ireland
8. Scotland
9. China
10.= Japan
10.= Nigeria

COOLING-OFF PERIOD
ENGLAND IN BELGIUM, EURO 2000 (*cat. no. 4929*)

DAVID'S GOLIATH MARCH TO WORLD CUP KOREA–JAPAN
ENGLAND 2001
(*cat. no. 5585*)
One man is about to produce one of the best ever performances in an England shirt, almost single-handedly dragging his team to the World Cup finals with a muscular, inspiring performance. And lashing in a freekick in the dying seconds.

ENGLAND TOURING TRIBES ARRIVE AT . . .

TOULOUSE, FRANCE '98 *(cat. no. 3609)*

Inside the City Hall a civic reception is interrupted by various 'Americans' come to look at the balcony. In reality, they are daring English Romeos who have come to exhibit messages of love for their hometown to those assembled in the Square below. Portsmouth ('Pompey'), as with most acts of capture, are first to the fore.

6. World Cup Tsunami

ARGIE BARGIE OVER TICKETS
ARGENTINA V. ENGLAND . . . V. IRELAND V. ITALY
NAPLES 1990 (*cat. no. 0081*)

UNIFORM FOR A WORLD CUP CAMPAIGN
ENGLAND PASSING BY STOCKPORT COUNTY 1990 (*cat. no. 0096*)
The World Cup exploits of Gazza and Gary (Lineker) down in Italy empower the schoolchildren
to wear the England kit as school uniform in the final weeks of term.

TWO YOUNG WOMEN IN PAINT EXCHANGE
ST DENIS, FRANCE '98 (*cat. no. 3909*)
The World Cup success of the hosts is creeping up on a
fairly unsuspecting nation.

JAPAN SURGE: JAPAN V. ARGENTINA
TOULOUSE, FRANCE '98 (*cat. no. 3554*)
The Asians are having their say, even if Argentina shall
run out winners.

ONE MAN AND HIS TEAM
FRANCE '98 (*cat. no. 3930*)
A team that shall rank amongst the best ever.
These players will go on to find fortune all over Europe.

141

CANCAN MEN
WORLD CUP FINAL,
FRANCE '98 (*cat. no. 3940*)
The French sense of the surreal
accompanies the most watched
match in history.

STILL WANDERING
IRELAND V. ROMANIA IN GENOA,
ITALIA '90 (*cat. no. 0085*)
Ireland are surprising themselves.

SCHOLES SHOT GOALBOUND
ENGLAND AT MARSEILLES, FRANCE '98 (*cat. no. 3586*)
The Tunisian challenge is put to rest with an incisive strike.

IN THE COURT OF THE KING
SCOTLAND V. BRAZIL, ST DENIS, FRANCE '98 (*cat. no. 3534*)
The Scots are handed the task of taking on the reigning World Champions in the opening game.

AN ENGLISH CROWD GATHERED IN THE SQUARE
ENGLAND AT TOULOUSE, FRANCE '98 (*cat. no. 3612*)
After the win in Marseilles, England have every reason to be confident against Romania.

JAPANESE GIRLS MAKE CONTACT
ENGLAND V. DENMARK, NIIGATA, KOREA–JAPAN 2002 (*cat. no. 5815*)
The locals of Niigata sign up with Hull and Wycombe.

JAPANESE GIRLS GET THE MEASURE OF ENGLAND
ENGLAND AT NIIGATA, KOREA–JAPAN 2002 (*cat. no. 5816*)

SHOCK-HORROR
UNFOLDS
JAPAN AT SAITAMA,
KOREA–JAPAN 2002
(*cat. no. 5863*)
The match versus
Belgium offers high
drama for the home
fans.

FACING THEIR FANS A SECOND TIME
IRELAND AT IBARAKI, KOREA–JAPAN 2002 (*cat. no. 5840*)
After the draw versus Cameroon in the afternoon sunshine, Ireland swap coasts
to face the might of the Germans. Who else shall they draw?

CAMEROONIE JOURNALIST
CAMEROON, KOREA–JAPAN 2002 (*cat. no. 5837*)
The African team are highly fancied this time round.

MEDIA INTEREST
IRELAND, KOREA–JAPAN 2002 (*cat. no. 5836*)
The Japanese, as hosts, are under pressure to perform.

TV PRESENTER ON THE LOOKOUT
KOREA–JAPAN 2002 (*cat. no. 6191*)

PERFECT ZEROS
JAPAN AT SAITAMA, KOREA–JAPAN 2002 (*cat. no. 5860*)

WHERE'S ROY K.?
IRELAND V. CAMEROON, KOREA–JAPAN 2002 (*cat. no. 5835*)
With the absence of England crowd-trouble, one story has
dominated the British and Irish press.

BBC THREE
ENGLAND V. DENMARK, NIIGATA, KOREA–JAPAN 2002
(*cat. no. 5943*)
The game is about to produce a remarkable English win and a
trouble-free 'conga' running the length and breadth of the
stadium. In the rain.

WHICH WAY TO LOOK?
JAPAN V. BELGIUM, SAITAMA, KOREA–JAPAN 2002 (*cat. no. 5862*)
The phantom of this opera is helped along.

BECKHAM BODYGUARD
ENGLAND V. SWEDEN, SAITAMA, KOREA–JAPAN 2002
(*cat. no. 5786*)
Beckham has made it to Japan, after weeks of physiotherapy. An
extended fanclub awaits his first appearance.

153

SVENGLAND LINE-UP
ENGLAND V. SWEDEN, SAITAMA, KOREA–JAPAN 2002 (*cat. no. 5780*)
The cool of the evening welcomes the north Europeans. Sven, now of England, faces his countrymen.

ANGLO SECTION
ENGLAND V. NIGERIA, OSAKA, KOREA–JAPAN 2002
(*cat. no. 5982*)
Barrow, Southampton, Torquay . . . all represented. So too
Beckham, who is captain. A draw will see England progress.

REAL END OF LINER
SAITAMA, KOREA–JAPAN 2002 (*cat. no. 5956*)

WAR BUS
ENGLAND V. SWEDEN
SAITAMA, KOREA–JAPAN 2002 (*cat. no. 5958*)
Waiting in the wings.

GOING TO THE MATCH ON THE BOX
BRAZIL V. TURKEY, SAITAMA, KOREA–JAPAN 2002
(*cat. no. 6111*)

BIG FELLAS

OSAKA, KOREA–JAPAN 2002 (*cat. no. 5985*)

New ranks of England support.

CAUTION ON THE BRIDGE

NIIGATA, KOREA–JAPAN 2002 (*cat. no. 5944*)

The English consider jumping.

WATER GUN

SAITAMA, KOREA–JAPAN 2002 (*cat. no. 5953*)

Waiting in the wings.

UP IN ARMS

JAPAN V. BELGIUM, SAITAMA, KOREA–JAPAN 2002 (*cat. no. 5866*)

The match versus Belgium offers great humour for the home fans.

157

Days When the Rains Came, Korea–Japan 2002, Japan v. Turkey, Miyagi

MAN WITH NEWSPAPER (*cat. no. 6046*)

HUNCHBACK WITH COCA COLA (*cat. no. 6053*)

TWO FANS WITH INSTRUCTIONS (*cat. no. 6056*)

ROWING FOR JAPAN (*cat. no. 6040*)

FACE OF . . . (*cat. no. 6074*)

フットボールを心から愛し、そして、2002年のあの忘れられない夏我
々を暖かく迎えてくれた—すべての日本人に贈る

スチュアート・ク

BOY WITH GIFT (*cat. no. 6060*)

MAN WITH FRENCH MANAGER (*cat. no. 6054*)

MOTHER & DAUGHTER & RAIN (*cat. no. 6073*)

COUPLE WITH FLAGS (*cat. no. 6058*)

To the Japanese who have embraced football and made us so terribly welcome in their country during the unforgettable summer of 2002.

Stuart Clarke

159

SIDES ARE DRAWN, KAMAKURA (*cat. no. 6102*)

On the Beach at Kamakura, Japan v. Japan, Korea–Japan 2002

BEACHED FOOTBALL (*cat. no. 6106*)

SAND LETS FLY (*cat. no. 6104*)

POINTS TO BE GAINED (*cat. no. 6103*)

SENSE OF VICTORY (*cat. no. 6109*)

COMING YOUR WAY (*cat. no. 6105*)

MANAGER'S
ROLE
(*cat. no. 6108*)

PLUCKY
PLAYER
(*cat. no. 6107*)

IRELAND WITH ATTACKING OPTIONS
IRELAND V. CAMEROON, NIIGATA, KOREA–JAPAN 2002 (*cat. no. 5831*)
Some time back in the cold war, North Korean soldiers crossed the Sea of Japan and seized a teenage couple necking on
the Niigata beach, to do what with them no one really knows. The couple split up but the lady lives on there.
Ireland put aside all distractions of 'Keane missing' to discover that without him the team is more than capable.

163

ENGLAND ATTACK ARGENTINA AT SAPPORO
SAPPORO, KOREA–JAPAN 2002 (*cat. no. 5791*)

The match is rightly hyped as the match of the tournament. England are looking for revenge for two World Cup exits
at the hands of the Argentinians, who have every reason to put three markers each on Owen and Beckham.
The match is played inside the Sapporo Dome, with its big black walls and roof blocking out the stars, the winds and
the rains to create a rarefied atmosphere.

ZIDANE ON THE SUBWAY
FRANCE AT KOREA–JAPAN 2002 (*cat. no. 6100*)
The world's best player gets across the secret of his success to the advert- and icon-loving Japanese.

Opposite page: TSUNAMI T-SHIRT
KOREA–JAPAN 2002 (*cat. no. 6130*)
Perhaps its the end of the world as we know it, or a teenage rampage. But the Japanese love of the slogan and their use of the western language is charmingly baffling. They are the masters of re-packaging something they like as almost their own. And they like cutesy things – so that it why they turn to supporting England. Well, that is to say: David Beckham.

A THIRD GOAL FOR . . .
ENGLAND V. DENMARK, NIIGATA, KOREA–JAPAN 2002 (*cat. no. 5810*)
The Danes have powered through the opening group stage . . . but England have arranged
for it to rain, then pour, plus they have an appointment with the next round.

DOUBLE TAKE
BRAZIL, KOREA–JAPAN 2002 (*cat. no. 6122*)
The Japanese view on nudity seems ambivalent. As does the Brazilians'.
The English, meanwhile, are passionately suppressed . . .

HOME OF ST GEORGE
THE ENGLISH LAKE DISTRICT DURING KOREA–JAPAN 2002
(*cat. no. 5779*)
Near Coniston a son has tarted up the farmhouse (whilst his
parents are away) in honour of the tournament on the other
side of the world.

PREGNANT PAUSE
TURKEY V. BRAZIL, SAITAMA, KOREA–JAPAN 2002
(*cat. no. 6091*)
The unfancied Turks meet Brazil twice in the tournament,
and come close each time, picking up support as they go.

IN AWE
JAPAN, KOREA–JAPAN
2002 (*cat. no. 5861*)
Japan amaze themselves
and the rest of the world
with their passion and
displays of emotion,
good humour and
understanding of the
game, on and off the
pitch. In summary: the
perfect breed of new
supporters.

RONALDINHO & CO. WALK OUT

BRAZIL V. ENGLAND, SHIZUOKA, KOREA–JAPAN 2002 (*cat. no. 5822*)

The table is cleared for a one-off 'who dares wins'. Pelé says before the game
that this 'should be the final' now that Argentina are out.

ENGLAND THE LIGHT
ENGLAND V. BRAZIL, SHIZUOKA, KOREA–JAPAN 2002 (*cat. no. 5821*)
In a stadium in a clearing in the forest, in view of Mount Fuji, a mysterious
atmosphere is conjured for the most important game so far.

JAPANESE BEAUTY, TICKETLESS
YOKOHAMA, KOREA–JAPAN 2002 (*cat. no. 5914*)

TOUTING CONVERSATION
BRAZIL V. TURKEY, SAITAMA, KOREA–JAPAN 2002 (*cat. no. 6128*)

NEARING OITA
MEXICO V. ITALY, OITA, KOREA–JAPAN 2002 (*cat. no. 6090*)
The Italians and Mexicans, both fancied, play out their group in the
far south. Brazil are beginning to look the best bet.

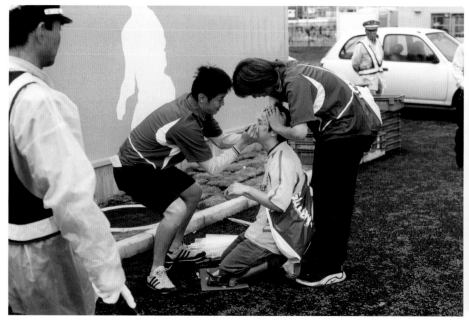

PLUCKED FROM THE HOARDING
BRAZIL V. TURKEY, SAITAMA, KOREA–JAPAN 2002 (*cat. no. 6135*)
The clamour to support Brazil is gathering momentum.

BECKHAM & SEAMAN MEET RONALDO
BRAZIL V. ENGLAND, SHIZUOKA, KOREA–JAPAN 2002 (*cat. no. 5969*)
It's almost the end of the line for Beckham and co.

SENDING IT DOWN THE PIPE
YEOVIL TOWN V. RUSHDEN AND DIAMONDS 2001 (*cat. no. 5348*)
The race from the Nationwide Conference to the English Football League is
again worthy stuff for live-TV coverage.

7. Back Home

ARMCHAIR FOOTBALL 2002 (*cat. no. 6199*)

DREAMING OF A BIG DAY
ROTHERHAM UNITED V. READING 2002
(*cat. no. 6279*)
'I was there' at Millmoor. But you have to
stay awake.

UPSTANDING
WEST HAM UNITED 2002
(*cat. no. 6309*)
Eyes look lovingly, or suspiciously, on
West Ham and their 'academy of
football'. They are bringing up the rear
of the English Premiership.

COMES TO LIFE
MANCHESTER CITY V. MANCHESTER
UNITED 2002 (*cat. no. 6438*)
Coronation Street aside, the Manchester
derby boasts the biggest drama.

OPTIMISTIC WOMAN
MANCHESTER CITY V. MANCHESTER
UNITED 2002 (*cat. no. 6421*)
It is the last Manchester derby, ever, at Maine
Road.

181

PRIZED MATCH
HUDDERSFIELD TOWN V. BARNSLEY
2002 (*cat. no. 6296*)
Derby tension is high.

SITTING COMFORTABLY
BARROW V. ACCRINGTON STANLEY
2002 (*cat. no. 6409*)
Barrow will beat the League leaders. But
he doesn't know that just yet.

SQUEEZE UP TO THE PALACE
CHELSEA V. ARSENAL 2002 (*cat. no. 6273*)
A childhood immersion in the big-match
atmosphere.

TIGHT TRIANGULAR PASSING
HUDDERSFIELD TOWN 2002
(*cat. no. 6295*)
Wadsworth's game plan came off. The
fans can go home happy. Set up for the
day. Proud all week. Someone will say 'I
love you' or 'Marry me' on the strength
of it.

SHEARER'S VOW
NEWCASTLE UNITED AT MANCHESTER UNITED 2002 (*cat. no. 6512*)
Thrashed many times at Old Trafford, a rejuvenated Shearer edges his United closer to the pace.

GOAL LOOKS ON

MANCHESTER CITY V. MANCHESTER UNITED 2002 (*cat. no. 6459*)

It could become a rout. It can become a rout. A rout would be to win even 1–0,
on this the last time at this very ground that the two shall meet.

CHELSEA V. ARSENAL IN THE VILLAGE
CHELSEA 2002 (*cat. no. 6271*)
International football (art) at its best.

HENRY ROLLS IT IN
ARSENAL AT LEEDS UNITED 2002 (*cat. no. 6323*)
What we didn't know at this stage, as Henry galloped around another bevy of useless tackles,
was just how good Arsenal were. Or the disarray of the home team.

CELEBRATIONS AMOK
BIRMINGHAM CITY V. LEEDS UNITED 2002 (*cat. no. 6246*)
The Blues, it is predicted, will be there or thereabouts (in the relegation zone) come
the end of the season. But they trounce Leeds with an electric-blue performance.

DAYS BEFORE THE WINTER SHUTDOWN
DERBY COUNTY 1992 (*cat. no. 0779*)
Talk on the streets is of moving away from The Baseball Ground for ever, while further afield, the talk is of English
football having an enforced winter break to recharge its batteries – as well as of other 'modernisations'.

THE LONE HUDDERSFIELD SUPPORTER
HUDDERSFIELD TOWN AT SOUTHEND UNITED 1991 (*cat. no. 0304*)
The lengths the Taylor Report went to after Hillsborough occasionally
provided a hammer to crack a nut. The one visiting supporter has been made
to sit a segregated distance away from the home congregation.

EAST CORNER FORTUNE
RANGERS 1992 (*cat. no. 0980*)
Rangers have upped the stakes and lifted a multi-million pound roof
onto their upper tier. Celtic will try and catch them.

8. *Final Matches at Favourite Old Grounds*

KEEPING THE HOMERS OUT
HULL CITY 2002 (CAT. NO. 6537)
Three years after a lock-out – the club being in receivership and a match away from extinction – Hull are now ready for their last game at troubled Boothferry Park. The Kingston Communications Stadium is ready and awaiting upwards of 25,000 attendances. It is bedecked in mauves and the very latest in stadium design. Hull as a club and as a city has set out their stall. There is no turning back for the Third Division Club (with the Premiership facilities).

TAKE THE CHILDREN AWAY
FULHAM V. LEICESTER CITY 2002 (*cat. no. 5690*)
Just as they are getting used to 'The Cottage' as home, they are
being told they have to leave.

BOY FINDS AL FAYED IN SPACE
FULHAM 2002 (*cat. no. 5685*)
The billionaire chairman savours the last game.

TWO BUCKETS SPARE
FULHAM 2002 (*cat. no. 5691*)

GOING OUT ON A HIGH
FULHAM 2002 (*cat. no. 5689*)
The crowd file away not
knowing whether they are to
return here, to a whole new
stadium after several years
redevelopment, or to some
other site.

ANOTHER EASY GAME FOR . . .
BOBBY ROBSON
SPORTING LISBON AT
MILLWALL 1993
(*cat. no. 1211*)
It's been a long and
distinguished career of
appointments. And one sacking –
at Fulham.

BOY WITH A HORN
FULHAM 2002 (*cat. no. 5684*)

TIME TO DELIVER
FULHAM V. LEICESTER CITY 2002 *(cat. no. 5700)*
Season's end – and so too the last ever game at Craven Cottage. A team costing some tens of millions is being fielded
on a (supposed) shabby old ground from yesteryear. Leicester City provide a modest send-off, having already been
relegated.

BOLTON SOCIAL
BOLTON WANDERERS V. PRESTON NORTH END AT CARDIFF 2001 (*cat. no. 5500*)
The Wanderers have flopped at this stage before. But today they have time to stop for a chat.
The Premiership awaits them a second, or is it a third, time?

ERIC TIES HIS SHOELACES AGAIN
MANCHESTER UNITED V. LIVERPOOL AT WEMBLEY 1996 (*cat. no. 2389*)
'The Cantona Final'. Otherwise undistinguished, for all McManaman's posturings.

NORWICH CITY V. BIRMINGHAM CITY
THE MILLENNIUM STADIUM, CARDIFF 2002 (*cat. no. 5717*)
Norwich have crept into the play-offs, then the semis, ousting Wolves, and finally to Cardiff where they take the game
to Birmingham. Amidst an unprecedented blaze of colour and gold-sequined cowboy hats. Even if Birmingham snatch
it in the penalty shoot-out.

WATFORD'S TRIUMPH OVER BOLTON WANDERERS
WEMBLEY 1999 (*cat. no. 4445*)
Newly promoted Watford have crept into the play-offs, then the semis, ousting Birmingham, and finally to Wembley
where they totally belittle Bolton amidst a flood of gold.

A DATE AT THE LAST MATCH AT BURNDEN PARK
BOLTON WANDERERS V. CHARLTON ATHLETIC 1997 (*cat. no. 3065*)
Everyone is here. Or almost everyone.

NEW HOME ON THE HORIZON
HUDDERSFIELD TOWN V. BRADFORD CITY 1994 (*cat. no. 1416*)
Huddersfield dominated English football during the early Herbert Chapman era, between the wars. Alfred McAlpine has
another treat in store a stone's throw up the road . . .

HOW CAN BOLTON STOP THEM?
BOLTON WANDERERS V. ARSENAL 2003 (*cat. no. 6680*)

Bottom versus top. The one trying to stave off the awful and quite likely relegation, whilst the free-scoring visitors looking to keep their noses ahead of Manchester United in the race for the title. Trailing by two goals with minutes remaining you would think it a lost cause. But the Wanderers have some flare and firepower of their own in Jay-Jay Okocha and Youri Djorkaeff. A match which turns out to decide the title, and keep Bolton in the Premiership.

214

WRIGHT DEMANDS HIS TALLY
ARSENAL V. NEWCASTLE UNITED 1994 (*cat. no. 1662*)
Cole waits up the other end for his chance. Wright won't wait for his. Two types of player, one goal. Highbury will
eventually be sold off, but the historic, listed side stands kept on for luxury flat redevelopment, with, between them, a
Highbury Park for walking the dog and sunbathing.

215

KING FOR A DAY
NEWCASTLE UNITED 1993 (*cat. no. 1162*)
Andy Cole's arrival at Newcastle is nothing short of a revelation. What would the Toon do without him should ever he be sold on? He came to them, they surely have a right to keep him.

LOOKING UP
SUNDERLAND 1996 (*cat. no. 2777*)
Season drawing to a close at old Roker Park. The mornings of the young supporters lives.

THE DISTINGUISHED ONE AWAITS A SECOND CHANCE
SUNDERLAND V. ARSENAL 2000 (*cat. no. 4987*)
Niall Quinn is poised on the halfway line, on-side, fancying his
chances in a sprint finish against his former employers. He wants
to finish it off. Sunderland are already in the lead. This is the
Stadium of Light, built on the banks of the Wear.

HAND IN MOUTH

LIVERPOOL V. ARSENAL 2001 (*cat. no. 5452*)

'Murdered' for much of the match by a superior team, Liverpool come late with two goals to steal the Cup.

THE KIPPAX ROARS
MANCHESTER CITY V. MANCHESTER UNITED 2002 (*cat. no. 6478*)
The City claims that if all other matches are not won this season (which the majority of them are not),
this one victory will make for a great year.

ROONEY SHADOWED IN THE PARK
EVERTON V. LIVERPOOL 2003 (*cat. no. 6650*)
A mercurial son is born unto these streets. But the streets have two sides.

TENDERNESS AT MAINE ROAD
MANCHESTER CITY V. SOUTHAMPTON 2003
(*cat. no. 6700*)
The last ever game at Maine Road is something special.
Even the coldest of shoulders will not be turned today.

WITH A GOLD HANDBAG
MANCHESTER CITY V. SOUTHAMPTON 2003
(*cat. no. 6702*)

IN ANTICIPATION
MANCHESTER CITY V. SOUTHAMPTON 2003
(*cat. no. 6704*)

HEADS AND MASCOTS
MANCHESTER CITY V. SOUTHAMPTON 2003
(*cat. no. 6708*)

LEAVING IT TO THE LAST GAME
MANCHESTER CITY V. SOUTHAMPTON 2003 (*cat. no. 6712*)

WITH BUGGS BUNNY
MANCHESTER CITY V. SOUTHAMPTON 2003
(*cat. no. 6705*)
Sun and showers.

223

GOATER'S SLOW WALK TO PASTURES NEW
MANCHESTER CITY V. SOUTHAMPTON 2003 (*cat. no. 6717*)
If there is to be one thing the last game at Maine Road will be remembered for, it will be the departure of the original 'badly drawn boy' – there is something about Sean Goater that is so very 'Manchester City'. He leaves the pitch to rapturous applause. The chanting of his name will drown the mass of post-match 'entertainment' well beyond the final curtain call.

PRIMITIVE CHALLENGE
ULLSWATER UNITED V. PENRITH RANGERS 2003 (*cat. no. 6648*)
Down in the valley, it's a battle for Second Division status.

EARLY FORMATIONS
ULLSWATER UNITED V. PENRITH RANGERS 2003 (*cat. no. 6647*)

228

ON BLACK CAT TIME/THE END IS NIGH

SHREWSBURY TOWN V. CARLISLE UNITED 2003 (*cat. nos 6670, 6671, 6672, 6673, 6674, 6675*) The trapdoor is almost open. Shrewsbury – who have had one of their finest hours this season in becoming giant-killers over Everton and Wayne Rooney – suddenly find themselves on the precipice looking at non-League football. Carlisle, who always escape, have to be beaten, tonight, in this very hour of asking.

BLADES FELLED BY WOLVES
WOLVERHAMPTON WANDERERS V. SHEFFIELD UNITED, CARDIFF MILLENNIUM STADIUM 2003 (*cat. no. 6752*)
The result would be hard to predict. However, the feeling had been that, come the final hour of asking, Wolves would blow it, as usual, and United would come good. So will United make it to the Premiership? This First Division play-off fixture could be viewed as the most important game in football, worth the biggest purse . . .

GIANT TIME
WOLVERHAMPTON WANDERERS V. SHEFFIELD UNITED,
CARDIFF MILLENNIUM STADIUM 2003 (*cat. no. 6751*)
This time Wolves fulfil the legend.

PREMIERSHIP ON VIEW AT THE COMMONS
HOUSE OF PARLIAMENT, WESTMINSTER 2003
(*cat. no. 6730*)
The biggest prize in football is a ticket to the Premiership and as much as £30,000,000 – and risen by the time you have read this.

TOO MUCH TO BARE
CARDIFF CITY V. QUEENS PARK RANGERS, CARDIFF MILLENNIUM
STADIUM 2003 (*cat. no. 6741*)
For City to fail on home turf would feel like there was no home to return
to. An unaccustomed quiet descends on the Welsh congregation.

BIRD'S EYE VIEW
CARDIFF CITY V. QUEENS PARK RANGERS, CARDIFF MILLENNIUM
STADIUM 2003 (*cat. no. 6741*)
Now in the streets the girls are dressed in their Sunday best.

SHEPHERDS BUSH TELEGRAM
QUEENS PARK RANGERS V. CARDIFF CITY, CARDIFF MILLENNIUM
STADIUM 2003 (*cat. no. 6743*)
The club have been through the mill, whilst their London neighbours
have prospered. Much could be said today.

GRAB ON TO THE ONES YOU LOVE
CARDIFF CITY V. QUEENS PARK RANGERS, CARDIFF MILLENNIUM
STADIUM 2003 (*cat. no. 6744*)
The goal is scored. It's a defining moment in your lifetime that
you simply have to share with the people who mean most to you.

GIRL ON THE EDGE OF HER SEAT
ARSENAL 2002 (*cat. no. 5747*)
No better thrill from growing up in
England. The Cup is hers.

LAST DAY ON THE SHELF
TOTTENHAM HOTSPUR 1994
(*cat. no. 1431*)

Me in My Time

My dad was off to a football match and I was two weeks overdue. He turned back when he met the doctor coming the other way – he could see the replay. The match was drawn 0–0.

And so it was. That's how I like to think of it, of being born into a footballing world. My father's fascination with football may well have extended to his own father's – I have a picture of my grandfather captaining Berkhamsted Town in 1905. Recently the same Town, but without him, got to the final of the FA Vase at Villa Park and many people I'd known all my life, if only by sight, were there on one large terrace. So like a dream. I look at that picture of my grandfather and the other players – he's the only one without a moustache – with intrigue. The power of a photograph is that you are taken straight into a time and place, as if you were there. It is as if the photo is telling the absolute truth. All the other things that my grandfather went through in his life and how he looked at other times (possibly with a moustache) fall away and that single photograph dominates the imagination.

That photo takes me right back to the turn of the century and almost to the birth of the organised game. Grandfather lived through all those times of scratched-up black-and-white showreel, seeing images like the silver horse clearing the pitch at Wembley and the Zeppelin going over the same ground a few years later. He was never around to be asked about these events and how he saw them in real time, but clutching that photo of him with the Berkhamsted Town ball I feel I am in touch with all of these events and times.

My dad was going off to Watford that day I was born. No surprise then that my family have supported Watford since then and that the club's yellow-gold is a special colour for me. When I see it in almost any context my heart jumps slightly. That's why I feel we are short-changed somewhat when our team turns up in a change of strip, sometimes completely needlessly. I have quizzed managers about this and they say it's sometimes at the whim of the bag man. I thought it was all a great plot by some super-efficient, conniving, world-conquering marketing department that probably has little feeling for the game. How suspicious I can be. Some bag man has probably sniffed the kits and thought, 'This one smells fresher for the boys.' And out they run.

I like the 'real' values inherent in the game: the colours; the name of the teams themselves; their League position; their current form; and the thought as the two teams run out of the pitch that, irrespective of form, one of these teams or sets of players who you weigh up position-for-position shall very possibly emerge victor over the other.

Amazing! Particularly exciting are those games where there has to be a winner. And this is the attraction of the knock-out cup. So when Berkhamsted Town, who have done nothing all century since Grandfather, get a run in the Amateur (semi-professional) Cup and get through to the semi-final stage 322 miles north versus Bedlington Terriers in Northumberland, as they did in 2001, I get excited.

Imagine that day in March as I drove across from my new home in the Lake District to the old industrial town north of Newcastle. The locals there hadn't ever heard of Berkhamsted; their Bedlington Terriers always do well in this cup, as well as always winning their League. They couldn't even pronounce the name. '*Berkhmasted* who?' And then I watched my Berkhamsted maul these mighty Terriers by simply outplaying them in every department and in every way, 322 miles from their home.

And I took some photographs to boot because I had to play my part in the carry-on.

It's been documented before, but I'll say it again. My dad built a full-sized goal in our back garden when we were young and all the kids came round to play. That had a profound effect on me. So did the fact that all the 'London children' from the Children's Country Holiday Home that came to stay with us throughout the 1960s were from the Chelsea and Battersea areas.

From a young age, therefore, I was made to feel that it is right to look after others less fortunate than yourself. That it is only right that Dad should want to nip off to the football if he has half the chance, even when Mum is giving birth. And that the baby is born into the colour of its local football team whether he or she likes it or not.

Later on, when I was choosing a career path and had grown tired of the Falklands War, I started hitch-hiking, knowing that the milk of human kindness was out there, in various guises. In the cab of a lorry, or in the passenger seat of a car, I found the one same starting-point to most conversations: the town you come from and the fate of its football team. I realised that football is more powerful than war. Even the squaddies who gave me lifts (because they too hitch-hiked) were more interested in their team and the quirks of its ground than 'matches abroad'.

Football, I say with great pride, will be the first thing played or organised once whatever war has stopped. Football was what British and German soldiers played on Christmas Day during a truce in the First World War. I think of this and immediately want to be taken to Brighouse and hear the Rastrick Brass Band in the frost on some street corner to get that really, really shivery feeling I only feel in this country.

I'm thus taken full-circle to that photo of my grandfather's Berkhamsted team. His brothers were in the First World War. One or even two never returned. I'm apt to think of them playing football out on some foreign field. Still.

The photography I take wants to be colourful and contemporary and say to every man and his dog: we are all part of this and we all play our part. Occasionally it's beautiful (the highest ideal) and mostly it's ludicrous and funny. The photographs I take say with great authority, 'This is the vital moment', whilst often taking a moment when nothing much is happening and there is no 'star' apparent. People say that the ordinary people, the fans, are my stars. And it's kind of nice that they remain unknown and nameless, for the moment one starts thrusting them into the spotlight they might become less the unsuspecting stars and show-stealers.

I like the underdog. I like to notice things that others may overlook. I never use a telephoto lens. My approach has always been to use a 'standard' lens – which is to say that when a picture looks like it was taken three metres away, it was. This means confronting the people in my pictures. Getting up close. I like that intimacy even if they never actually know they have had their photo taken. It's not just that I want to get one over on them, but because if you go, 'Look this way', it changes the very thing (of beauty) that you saw in them, and the photo is void. Another thing about the camera and my approach is that I always print the whole negative, piece of film or picture – I never crop things out or change anything. It's almost as if once the picture has been taken it becomes something sacred to me. And yet, if I had just moved the camera a touch to the left or up or down, the picture would have appeared very different and in the crowd and group scenes certain people would have then been out of shot and others in. The whole of the history recorded would have been different!

However, and I might add, in a footballing context, crowds have a habit of trying to do exactly the same thing time over and be in exactly the same spot week upon week. In the days of terraces (which still exist at Berkhamsted) people tended to try and find the same spot every match – whatever the weather and their mood – instead of trying out loads of different positions around the ground, which would seem the more interesting thing to do. Which is what I do. But I am always in the same spot really, which is to say in football's sacred ground.

SUNSET OVER SPRINGFIELD PARK
WIGAN ATHLETIC 1990 (*cat. no. 201*)
The greatest spectacle of any? A game that will always be with us . . .

The Great and the Good

DR TARA BRABAZON, SENIOR LECTURER, COMMUNICATION AND CULTURAL STUDIES, SCHOOL OF MEDIA COMMUNICATION AND CULTURE, MURDOCH UNIVERSITY, AUSTRALIA

'Although best known for the remarkable crowd shots, I have always preferred Stuart Clarke's photographs of people and places in the corners of sport. The "Neon Girls" (page 14) serving fried food to Tranmere Rovers fans shows his skill in making the ordinary events of a sporting life unexpected and surprising. The teased hair, glossed lips and kohl-lined eyes mark these women as part of the game, not servants to it. For Stuart Clarke, women are part of football and its community, and he provides a record of their role.'

MARK RADCLIFFE, RADIO 1 DJ

'I was once at Maine Road when the great City keeper Joe Corrigan approached the North Stand crowd and enquired of someone in the front row what the time was. It's been a long time since one of our goalies has found himself similarly bored due to inaction, but "Goalkeepers' View of the Crowd" (pages 28–9) gives some impression of how close to the emotional outpourings of the crowd the men between the sticks are.

'What a day. And in the religious frenzy and fervour, the lame really do appear to have thrown down their crutches and walked. As this was the day we returned to the big time, there's a more than tempting resurrection motif here, but I'll resist. However that day we did believe that Joe Royle could turn water if not into wine, then almost certainly Strongbow. What a day.'

DR STEVE REDHEAD, SENIOR LECTURER, COMMUNICATION AND CULTURAL STUDIES, MANCHESTER AND AUSTRALIA

'Stuart Clarke's soccer crowd fan photos are unique. The amazement in being a football fan is always there. "Goalkeepers' View of the Crowd" (pages 28–9) was taken of delirious Manchester City fans at Ewood Park, Blackburn, during their 4–1 win against Rovers. Despite the victory, for much of the match City had been outplayed. The fans are cheering in sheer disbelief rather than joy. City, unbelievably, were promoted at the end of the game.'

SANDY REID, AMBLESIDE

'"On the Bus With the Cup" (page 32). After nine years as barren as a biblical famine, Celtic, under the guidance of Wim "Willy Wonka" Jansen begin to find their stride and at last overtake the ageing, stumbling blue machine that roars out of Govan.

'There may be wobbles and woe to come in next few seasons, but the journey these Bhoys are embarking upon will ultimately lead them to the very edge of footballing utopia in Seville, albeit with a new conductor named O'Neill.'

JOHN MOTSON, BBC TV AND RADIO COMMENTATOR

'This photo, "Reporting from the Ground" (pages 42–3), did more for my image than I could have imagined. It has also made the sheepskin coat a cult garment.

'The amount of people who ask where was it and when . . . I tell the story about the localised snowstorm – always a good start for after-dinner speeches. I have a big pile of it in postcard form – thanks to Stuart – which I use for special occasions and as thank yous. Terrific.'

JOHN WILLIAMS, DIRECTOR, CENTRE FOR FOOTBALL RESEARCH, UNIVERSITY OF LEICESTER

'"The Kop" (page 43) depicts a rather serious and sober-looking standing Liverpool Kop, post-Hillsborough. This is a long way from Arthur Hopcraft's memorable depiction of the Kop in the early 1970s: "When the crowd surges at a shot or a collision near a corner flag a man or a boy, and sometimes a girl, can be lifted off the ground in the crush, as if by some massive, soft-sided crane and dangled about for minutes on end." It's dangling days were now through, although, as the guy to the right confirms, this new pacified and more orderly Kop was still no media pussy. Now seated, the Kop still struggles to capture the aura of the glory years – but then so does the Liverpool team.'

WILSON FAMILY, BOLTON

'"Family" would be a better title than "Friends" (page 50): the photo shows me, my wife, two daughters (thumbs up), brother-in-law, nephew and niece. My wife and I "dated" in the embankment in the early '70s. This was also my children's first season watching the Wanderers. To some it was the end of an era at Burnden, to the younger ones the beginning of their support.

'All are now season ticket holders and travel from Lancaster, Manchester and Aylesbury to watch the Wanderers. Even university choices revolved around the proximity to the Reebok Stadium. The photo constantly reminds us of that fantastic last game and the Reebok is now the venue where the family regularly reunites.'

PHILIP FRENCH, HEAD OF COMMUNICATIONS, FA PREMIER LEAGUE

'In "New Headlines to be Making" (page 59) the Pompey faithful welcome their heroes back in true ticker-tape style after being robbed of victory in the FA Cup semi-final against Liverpool. It was a roller-coaster season of heartbreak and near misses for the Pompey team after just failing by a whisker to get promoted, losing out to West Ham. But the club and Harry have perhaps had their revenge and with the Bald Eagle at his side the Pompey chimes will once again be ringing out at the top level of English football. Play Up Pompey!'

RT HON. LORD CLARK OF WINDERMERE

'"Fans Storm Their Heaven" (page 61). What memories. I was there. The previous month, Carlisle had played at Wembley for the first time in front of 77,000 fans. Now we were Third Division Champions. The First Division beckoned us!

'It was not to be. We dropped straight back and since then have been fighting simply to stay in the League. We even needed our on-loan goalkeeper, Jimmy Glass, scoring deep into injury-time to keep us up.

'During those dark days, Carlisle returned to Wembley and went to Cardiff and now in England's football outpost we believe we are on our way back.'

STAN TIPPINS, TOUR MANAGER FOR MOTT THE HOOPLE, SIMPLE MINDS AND OTHERS

'"Hops & Cider Reviver" (page 62). Stan Tippins has supported Hereford United for over 50 years, on a roller-coaster ride from their Southern League days, up to the old Second Division and back down into the Conference. His greatest moment came with United's election to the Football League, at a time when it was a closed shop. His dream now is to see United become a Community Club again and regain their place in the league – the great Hereford fans deserve nothing less.'

STU FORSTER, PRESS PHOTOGRAPHER

'Whenever I see TV footage or Stuart's picture of "Going Down At Roker" (page 70), it brings back mixed emotions. I had just started in press photography. I was at pitch-side, behind the goal just obscured in Stuart's picture. It shows Liam O'Brien turning to celebrate after curling the ball over the wall and scoring the winning goal in a 2–1 win, the first at the Mackems for many a year. After the initial moment of disbelief, O'Brien then legged it over towards the Newcastle fans to celebrate. I'd managed to rattle off 20-odd frames on the boss's ancient Nikon F3 camera before realising I hadn't checked to see if the film had wound on . . . and it hadn't. Whey, ye bugger . . .

'I'm still a press photographer, happy to say.'

MARK LAWRENSON, CHIEF FOOTBALL PUNDIT, BBC TELEVISION AND RADIO

'We live in a world of instant images from around the world, brought to us via satellite television, but the best images for me are pictorial. Football images are many, but capturing the moment isn't just about the winning goal – for me it's the match and "everything" that encapsulates the memories of such.

'Stuart Clarke's masterpiece is an excellent work covering every aspect of the game we love, my favourite being the "Maxwell House" (page 82) picture from the club that I managed briefly – Oxford United. It evokes many memories for me, both good and bad, but isn't that football?'

RICHARD SCUDAMORE, CHIEF EXECUTIVE, FA PREMIER LEAGUE

'"A Test of Speed" (page 92–3) captures it all: a packed ground, full of supporters; 22 players, all of them moving; the attackers homing in on the precious goal; defenders racing to cover; the referee at full tilt getting into position; the keeper in two minds – do I stay or do I move? You can go back to this photo time and again and find something new. It should be re-titled "Essence of the Game".'

GRAHAM SPIERS, WRITER

'As a sportswriter I have savoured some of the great football homes around Britain. And here's the deepest truth of that statement: I include Gayfield Park, Arbroath, the subject of "Entrance-Fee Review" (page 100), as well as Celtic Park, Glasgow, in this category, because a football team's home has its own individual enchantment. Gayfield Park, built right on the seashore, is so close to the crashing waves that one of their supporters once told me "you can almost reach out and catch a haddock with your bare hands" during storm-lashed winter Saturdays.'

GRAHAM BEAN, FOOTBALL ASSOCIATION COMPLIANCE OFFICER

'"Blood Red Road End" (page 102–3) or the "Ponty End", as it is locally known, has been the symbol of Barnsley Football Club as long as I can remember. As a lad, every time you went to the tarn, the bright red walls of Oakwell could clearly be seen from the windows of the bus as you passed by, despite the fact that it was a good 300 yards from the road. Every lad in Barnsley wanted to see what was on t'other side and when they did they were "Reds" forever.'

LANCE HARDY, ASSISTANT EDITOR, *FOOTBALL FOCUS*

'This scene, "Crack at Belle Vue" (pages 104–5), could be anywhere. That's the beauty of Stuart's work. In fact it's Doncaster during the club's days in the old Fourth Division. It holds special memories for me, as my first ever Football League match was Doncaster Rovers versus Aldershot, back in September 1976.

'For a while, of course, league football was locked away for both clubs and this old gate always reminded me of that fact, but 2003 has witnessed a Rovers return and a Shots revival too, so this old photograph now also brings new hope for tomorrow.

'But it will always take me back to my yesterdays and Belle Vue at the time when I was first getting hooked by this wonderful game.

'Thanks for the memories, Stuart.'

NICK BARNES, BBC RADIO NEWCASTLE

'You can smell football in "Where the Team are Briefed" (page 109). It reminds me of the years I spent covering Carlisle United in the Second and Third Divisions in the 1990s, when I would spend a fair amount of my working day at Brunton Park in the corridors and offices below the haphazard main stand waiting for interviews, chatting with staff and players.

'But the dressing-room was special. Somewhere it felt a privilege to be allowed. A secret inner sanctum that very few ever see. There's an aura in a dressing-room which embodies football. This photograph encompasses it. The liniment, the bandages, the towels, the kit lying on the bench, and above all . . . the pitch . . . on the wall . . . the blackboard where the dreams are drawn and then rubbed out. There's an enchantment about this photograph that captures the thrill I felt for football as a boy, and the association I have with it now as a commentator. It reminds me why the lower divisions are so important. And I just love the teapot. You can smell the tea.'

DAVID DENT, CARLISLE UNITED, COVENTRY CITY

'It is his interest in football at every level that makes Stuart Clarke's collection so special. Although I spent my entire working life serving the professional game, it is pictures such as "Green and Pleasant Landing" (pages 112–13) of Ambleside football ground that take me back to where it all began in the Westmorland League. In its own way, football on this field every Saturday afternoon is just as important to the players as that other match at Old Trafford. And it's arguable that the setting is more attractive!'

JON CHAMPION, ITV COMMENTATOR

'From the top of Grimsby's Findus Stand you feel like you can see to the end of the earth. No sane individual gets this high – only television commentators and intrepid photographers. I love "Ebb & Flow" (page 124) for its illustration of the straitjacket that is 4–4–2, for the intrusion of the maritime world, and for showing in all its glory the oldest grandstand at an English league ground, built in 1901 and untouched by progress.'

KEVIN MOORE, DIRECTOR, NATIONAL FOOTBALL MUSEUM, PRESTON

'"Goalscoring Thoroughbred" (page 126). This man was the bargain of the century when bought by Tranmere from Real Sociedad for £250,000 in 1991. Johnny King, the Tranmere manager, had been trying to sign Aldo since he began his playing career with South Liverpool. As a Tranmere fan, what I loved about Aldo, both as a player and as a manager, was his intense burning passion for the game, both on and off the pitch. He lives and breathes the game like a fan.'

HENRY WINTER, CHIEF FOOTBALL WRITER, *DAILY TELEGRAPH*

'"England Attack Argentina at Sapporo" (pages 164–5). This space-age baseball stadium was the dramatic setting for some very old-style emotions and a compelling footballing drama. For David Beckham, this wonderful victory over Argentina was all about redemption, all about banishing the ghosts that had stalked him since his France '98 dismissal. The Argentinians tried to put him off but Beckham kept his nerve and his cathartic penalty made the world look right again. Having celebrated the win with a dignity that contrasted with Argentinian crowing in France, Beckham and the players headed to the tunnel. Away from the cameras and the world's watching eye, they charged to the dressing-room, screaming delightedly, "That was for St-Etienne!" A memorable occasion.'

MARTIN HAYMAN, ENGLISH BANKER IN JAPAN

'"A Third Goal for . . ." (pages 168–9). Most of us expats had been fearing the influx of England's infamous fans more than the Japanese, but it was a joy to don club and national colours and join the exuberant hordes. After Sapporo the locals were won over, and the celebrations during the second half in Niigata became legendary. Baseball, the Japanese sporting preoccupation, was sidelined and for a few weeks Japanese, English, Irish, Germans, Brazilians, even Americans, thronged Tokyo bars in a wonderfully united reverie of football.'

MARTIN SHERIFF, WATFORD FAN, LEIGHTON BUZZARD

'The day of "Watford's Triumph Over Bolton Wanderers" (pages 208–9) my family were renting a cottage at a place called Craigievar, which is about 35 miles from Aberdeen Despite weeks of effort to get flights back to London on the day of the match, I settled for two return train tickets from Edinburgh to Kings Cross. The problem was that the train would leave Edinburgh at 7 a.m. and we were 150 miles and over 3 hours away across the mountain roads via Braemar. I woke my son Andrew before 3 a.m. and we were on the road to the station by 3.15. The train ran well and we arrived at Kings Cross with our large banner aloft.

'The buzz as we walked to the ground was tremendous. I had been there in 1984 to witness the Cup final defeat at the hands of Everton, but this was not like that occasion. This was much more important than a cup final. This guaranteed a season in the Premier League. The game flew by and, courtesy of goals from Allan Smart and Nicky Wright, we had earned our place at the top table.

'We arrived in Edinburgh at around midnight and as we drove back over the mountains, the American DJ on Radio 2 (it was the only reception we could get) read out a request at 3 a.m. from someone associated with Watford Football Club for any supporters still travelling home from the match . . . truly amazing!'

MICHAEL CUNNAH, CHIEF EXECUTIVE WEMBLEY (THE NATIONAL) STADIUM

'New season, new hope, old faithful. Niall Quinn's winner against Arsenal in the first match of the 2000–01 season allowed Sunderland fans to believe that their team had finally arrived in the "big time". Further proof, as if any was needed, came from the magnificent new Stadium of Light, the best in the Premiership. Even though "The Distinguished One Awaits a Second Chance" (pages 218–19) shows our superhero with hands on knees, gasping for breath, Quinny was special – he allowed us to dream. On this day life was great.'

CLARE TOMLINSON, SKY SPORTS TOUCHLINE REPORTER AND PRESENTER

'This was taken the morning after "The Last Day of The Shelf" (page 232) – a game I remember well. There was sadness that after all the fighting to preserve it from corporate boxes, it was finally to be taken from us. But the day was a celebration of the best standing view in the country and this is a fitting epitaph.'

Acknowledgements

As well as the sponsors, the Great and the Good, the football clubs and administrators, and the unknown-soldier football fans, Stuart Clarke would like to thank the following:

WEMBLEY STEPS
ENGLAND 1999 (*cat. no. 4331*)
The National Stadium has history etched all over it. So much so that few can talk about its redevelopment dispassionately.

ABIGAIL JACOBS – are you OK?

AMBLESIDE, THE LAKE DISTRICT – the most beautiful place on earth.

BIG GED SCOTT – Midlands football journalist. Has had to reel in the bullshit in the quest for accuracy.

BILL CAMPBELL at Mainstream Publishing – for seeing the potential in this first book with you and pricing it generously for the people to enjoy.

CHROMAZONE of Gateshead – for all the large (touring) exhibition prints by which I have made my name over 14 years.

CONISTON FC – for letting Homes of Football sponsor them and making them put their names on the shirts and for very nearly almost winning the Championship with a pedigree of flair.

GLASTONBURY, READING FESTIVALS – rock on!!

IAN FENTON – if I first taught you about film, you have become the mentor now.

JACK THIE – it's not all about winning, but heck, we've never had a winner in the Clarke clan.

JIMMY, ROBIN AND CHRIS BROWN at Bridgend – you remind me how good it is to have neighbours, and thanks for the updates on Ullswater United FC, plus other goings-on in the valley where they filmed that 'sexed-up' programme, *The Lakes*!

JOHN HEXT, of Coniston – worked for us in Ambleside almost since we opened, when you yourself were 'a boy'.

KAREN CHAPMAN – helped get the PFA flag flying over Ambleside Museum and get us a direct line with Gordon Taylor every time.

LANCE HARDY of BBC Sports – who made a great impression (on me) with his TV production: a review of France '98 with the voice over by Jon Champion, which we still play in our gallery.

MARTIN HUDSON – who in a perfect world would have worked with us in making Homes of Football perfect . . . now his brother has got in on the act a bit!

MARY CLARKE – I have the greatest admiration of all, for you.

MATTHEW ASHTON – Shrewsbury born and bred and kindred-spirit photographer. Had to watch with lump in throat 'my' Carlisle dump 'his' Shrewsbury out of the League.

NISHA – the great god Pan serving up superior eclectic tastes in that Kendal Mint Cake town.

NUTTER with the hammer, September '98 – WE are still standing.

PAUL ALDERSON – Carlisle fan, who also has time for the White Stripes and Bruce Springsteen.

PHILIP FRENCH – Chichester boy made good-ish. Thank you for everything.

READING MUSEUM – for taking the show at a time to coincide with the book launch and for being so darn up for it all.

SANDY REID – a servant to the cause, even if – or because – a Celt. He was the one in Seville with the sombrero.

SUNDERLAND MUSEUM – for handling the touring show at short notice and at a difficult time and having it look so grand, as indeed it is.

UNCLE ALAN AND AUNTIE PAT – don't you ever die, you last of the old Clarkes, fielding for Berkhamsted and Selsey.

WARD PHILIPSON of Gateshead – for all the film-processing. Never, since 1990, did you once uck it up.

WICKED WITCH OF THE SOUTH – you had your chance, but the north wasn't taken in . . . and finally: SWEEP, as in Sooty, for lending a hand.

PITCH TURNED SKY BLUE
MANCHESTER CITY V. SOUTHAMPTON
2003 (*cat. no. 6718*)

England Scotland Republic of Ireland Northern Ireland Wales Brazil Germany Italy France Turkey Liverpool Arsenal Chelsea Everton Manchester United Middlesbrough Blackburn Rovers Tottenham Hotspur Newcastle United Leeds United Southampton Manchester City Fulham Aston Villa Birmingham City Sunderland Charlton Athletic West Ham United West Bromwich Albion Bolton Wanderers Portsmouth Leicester City Norwich City Watford Nottingham Forest Reading Sheffield United Coventry City Rotherham United Wolverhampton Wanderers Burnley Crystal Palace Derby County Gillingham Wimbledon Millwall Preston North End Walsall Bradford City Ipswich Town Grimsby Town Stoke City Sheffield Wednesday Brighton & Hove Albion Wigan Athletic Oldham Athletic Cardiff City Bristol City Crewe Alexandra Queens Park Rangers Brentford Blackpool Chesterfield Luton Town Tranmere Rovers Wycombe Wanderers Port Vale Northampton Town Stockport County Plymouth Argyle Barnsley Swindon Town Notts County Huddersfield Town Colchester United Peterborough United Cheltenham Town Mansfield Town Hartlepool United Rushden & Diamonds Bournemouth Torquay United Wrexham Kidderminster Harriers Cambridge United Scunthorpe United Lincoln City Bury Oxford United York City Southend United Hull City Shrewsbury Town Rochdale Macclesfield Town Leyton Orient Darlington Carlisle United Bristol Rovers Exeter City Boston United Swansea City Chester City Hereford United Workington Gretna Aylesbury United Bedlington Terriers Berkhamsted Town Taunton Town Barry Town Bangor City Coniston Ambleside United Ullswater United Barrow Rangers Celtic Hearts Dunfermline Athletic Hibernian Dundee Aberdeen Kilmarnock Livingston Partick Thistle Dundee United Motherwell Falkirk Inverness Caledonian Thistle St Johnstone Clyde Queen of South Ayr United Ross County St Mirren Arbroath Alloa Athletic Raith Rovers Stranraer Berwick Rangers Brechin City Forfar Athletic Dumbarton Cowdenbeath Airdrie United Hamilton Academicals Stenhousemuir East Fife Peterhead Albion Rovers Greenock Morton Stirling Albion Gretna Elgin City Montrose Queen's Park East Stirling Forres Mechanics Huntly Abbey Stadium Adams Road Aggborough Stadium Alderstone Road Anfield Ashton Gate Avenue Stadium Ayresome Park Baseball Ground Bay View Belle Vue Bescot Stadium Bloomfield Road Blundell Park Boghead Bootham Crescent Boothferry Park Borough Park Boundary Park Bower Fold Bramall Lane Brisbane Road Britannia Stadium Broadwater Brockville Brunton Park Buckingham Road Burnden Park Burslem Cappielow Carrow Road Celtic Park Christie Park City Ground Cliftonhill County Ground Craven Cottage Dean Court Deepdale Dell Den Dens Park Deva Stadium Douglas Park Dronfield East End Park Easter Road Eastville Edgar Street Edgeley Park Elland Road Elm Park Ewood Park Feethams Fellows Park Filbert Street Field Mill Firhill Fir Park Fratton Park Gay Meadow Gayfield Park Giant Axe Gigg Lane Glandford Park Goldstone Ground Goodison Park Gresty Road Griffin Park Haig Avenue Hampden Park Hawthorns High Park High Street Highbury Highfield Road Hillsborough Holker Street Home Park Huish Park Ibrox Stadium Irongate Ground JJB Stadium Kenilworth Road Kilbowie Park Kingsfield Road Layer Road Leeds Road Links Park Loftus Road London Road Love Street McAlpine Stadium McDiarmid Park Madejski Stadium Maine Road Manor Ground Meadow Lane Millennium Stadium Millmoor Molineux Moss Rose Nene Park Ninian Park Oak Tree Road Oakwell Old Trafford Ora Stadium Palmerston Park Head Parkside Road Pittodrie Plainmoor Plough Lane Portman Road Prenton Park Pride Park Priestfield Stadium Racecourse Ground Raydale Park Recreation Ground Reebok Stadium Riverside Rockingham Road Roker Park Roots Hall Rugby Park St Andrews St George's Lane St James' Park St Mary's Saltergate Sandy Lane Sealand Road Selhurst Park Shay Shepherdsbridge Sincil Bank Sixfields Spotland Springfield Park Stadium of Light Stamford Bridge Tannadice The Dell The Den The Hawthorns The Shay The Stadium The Valley Turf Moor Twerton Park Tynecastle Underhill University of Bath Upton Park Vale Park Valley Valley Parade Vetch Field Vicarage Road Victoria Ground Victoria Park Villa Park Walkers Stadium Watling Street Welfare Ground Wembley Whaddon Road White Hart Lane Windsor Park Going to the match Standing Seating Coach travel Sponsors Hoardings Turnstiles Corner-flags Disabled Stretchers Floodlights Mascots Shirts Boots Dugouts The Bench Tea-Rooms Burger Vendors Changing-Rooms Football Inflatables Tannoys Tunnels Exits Players Stewards First-Aid Commentators John Motson Referees Linesmen Managers Coaches Substitues Police Police Horses Police Dogs TV Coverage Radio Commentary BBC ITV Sport Radio Five Live Sky Sports Irish Football Scottish Football Welsh Football Women's Football Junior Football Playing-fields Icons Zidane Beckham Shearer McCoist Andy Cole Cantona Gascoigne Ronaldo Del Piero Vialli Keegan Bryan Robson Lineker Platt Waddle Graham Taylor Souness Martin O'Neill Dalglish George Graham Howard Wilkinson Joe Royle Jim Smith Alex Ferguson Sven-Goran Erickson Success Winning Losing Winners Losers Crying Laughing Singing Westmorland League Football League Nationwide Conference Nationwide League Premier League World Cup FA Cup Champions League